REAL CLASSROOM MANAGEMENT

Whose Job Is It?

Mark M. Jacobs
Nancy Langley

Rowman & Littlefield Education
Lanham, Maryland • Toronto • Plymouth, UK
2007

Published in the United States of America
by Rowman & Littlefield Education
A Division of Rowman & Littlefield Publishers, Inc.
A wholly owned subsidiary of The Rowman & Littlefield Publishing Group,
Inc.
4501 Forbes Boulevard, Suite 200, Lanham, Maryland 20706
www.rowmaneducation.com

Estover Road
Plymouth PL6 7PY
United Kingdom

British Library Cataloguing in Publication Information Available

Library of Congress Cataloging-in-Publication Data

Jacobs, Mark M., 1947–
   Real classroom management : whose job is it? / Mark M. Jacobs, Nancy
Langley.
      p. cm.
   Includes bibliographical references.
   ISBN-13: 978-1-57886-640-3 (hardback : alk. paper)
   ISBN-10: 1-57886-640-5 (hardback : alk. paper)
   ISBN-13: 978-1-57886-641-0 (pbk. : alk. paper)
   ISBN-10: 1-57886-641-3 (pbk. : alk. paper)
   1. Classroom management. 2. Education—Parent participation. 3.
Community and school. I. Langley, Nancy, 1952– II. Title.
   LB3013.J335 2007
   371.102'4—dc22

                                                            2007018095

⊗™ The paper used in this publication meets the minimum requirements
of American National Standard for Information Sciences—Permanence of
Paper for Printed Library Materials, ANSI/NISO Z39.48-1992.
Manufactured in the United States of America.

CONTENTS

INTRODUCTION

How do we turn ineffective classroom management around? How do we as educational leaders help our staff improve classroom behavior or at the very least increase learning without myriad interruptions from students who have not yet learned to focus? How can teachers effectively work with parents to ensure students receive an optimum learning experience? What is the role of the entire community when putting together a successful classroom management program?

We suggest that by utilizing five essential skills for school leaders (Langley & Jacobs, 2006) teachers and administrators can successfully interact with parents and the community as a whole to create an atmosphere where teachers are in control of the learning situation and students are productive. These five skills are only one tool needed to build a solid classroom management plan. Therefore, as we explore what makes a good classroom management plan, we must identify our skills and incorporate them in our daily business.

The five essential skills can be summed up as follows:

1. Insightfulness
2. Strong, positive interpersonal skills
3. Flexibility
4. Self-growth
5. Keeping in touch with the community

The first step in utilizing the five essential skills is recognizing that they all overlap each other. Proper utilization of these five skills will not provide a miracle cure for a less than perfect classroom management plan. However, it will help alleviate certain problems. For example, let us look at the first skill, the ability to be insightful. Knowing what lies ahead will enable a teacher to predict, to some degree, and work toward preventing a child's misbehavior in class.

What we suggest does take initial steps on behalf of the teacher. Good instruction requires work. All teachers, administrators, parents, and the school community recognize this fact. So what can we administrators do to foresee problems that our staff will run into, and how do we help them? The "how we help them" part is critical. Administrators know that a smaller class size will help, and we also know that simply removing certain students from your class will help balance the power of control in your favor.

However, we of course cannot just remove any "Tom, Dick, or Jane" from our classes when students act up. In this book we will explore the meaning of classroom management and the roles we all play in exacting this concept. The principle players are teachers, guidance counselors, all school-based administrators, central office administrators, consultants, instructors of university education courses, and the students enrolled in such programs. Of course, we cannot forget parents and the general public. In other words, everyone connected to a school has an important role in the overall classroom management.

Classroom management is a collaborative effort that affects the entire community. Whenever people interact, they must remember that, no matter how good their plans appear, at least some of their ideas will not be accepted by everyone. Personalities and differing points of views contribute to the success or failure of any plan. One plan does not fit all sizes. The information shared in this book will give the readers suggestions of plans that might work in their own settings. Some of the suggestions have proven to be quite successful in some settings and may be adaptable to other sites without change. Other suggestions might fit with a little tweaking here and there. Our intention in this work is to provide enough samples and data to help the readers put together a classroom management plan that is best for their situation.

When addressing the issue of classroom management, there should be a leader, but not an exclusive person who makes all the decisions. Each leader should be the model that sets examples as well as standards. In *Five Essential Skills for School Leaders: Moving from Good to Great* (Langley & Jacobs, 2006), a leader is defined as anyone who makes a decision that affects anyone other than himself or herself. Therefore, our leader is in fact a compilation of the administrators, the teachers, the parents, the community, and the students.

Classroom management. These two words conjure up different meanings for different people. Examining each separately, the word *classroom* most likely stirs up memories of a room filled with wall hangings that reflect the results of student efforts. There are desks with many children—some appear attentive and pleased to be there, others perhaps less enthusiastic. In the front of the room, we envision a teacher—a kindly, matronly woman much like our grandmothers or maybe a slightly less favorable memory of someone who more closely resembles Attila the Hun with a yardstick.

When we think about the word *management* we might envision a superior giving out orders and trying to run a smooth ship. Or, we might recall situations in which we were called upon to make decisions, to organize or plan for others as well as for our own personal direction.

Read (1996) defines management as the skillful use of means to accomplish a purpose. There is no mention of whether management is a sole or cooperative effort. Perhaps that is because it is a combination of both. Such is the case with classroom management. This is not an independent effort but a collaboration of ideas and actions. When we take the images we have created in our minds of both classroom and management and put them together, we might just find that we come up with an image that is different from the ones we created for each word independently.

In other words, when we look at classroom management, we should examine it as an idiom. Separately these words produce one set of images; together they take on a new meaning. No matter what image this word produces for each of us, it is most probable that at least some of our ideas are quite similar. However, because of the wide range of information one might associate with the term, the word *management* is apt to create a variety of many different interpretations.

When we think of the concept of management, do we envision large corporations headed by the kind faces of such moguls as the Donald Trumps of the world? Or, do we see ruthless tyrants such as Joseph Stalin? Is the goal to help others develop their positive leadership skills or to mimic the direction of the boss? What is the role of the manager? Is he someone in complete control? Is she conducting her efforts independently as a mere overseer of activities, or is she interacting with others? Does the word *management* refer to a means to discipline? Are there many issues that form one overall manager? How important is structure to forming our image?

Classroom management is a conglomeration of these images. There must be order. Order not only refers to a strong lesson plan and strictly structured rules of discipline but also includes the classroom atmosphere and setting. By this we mean that teachers should examine the layout of desks, other furniture, and educational resources or materials to ensure that they enhance the learning process rather than detract from it. A classroom that is not properly coordinated can have adverse effects on overall classroom management, resulting in lack of attention on the part of the students and thereby causing decline in academic success.

We can carry this further to the structure of the entire school. Hallways, staircases, and other common areas should allow for easy movement and good accessibility and provide an atmosphere where adult supervision is not impaired. The grounds of a school building should be as aesthetically pleasing as possible while offering child-friendly, safe, and secure surroundings. By this we mean one should ensure not only that the grounds do not have structures that might be dangerous for students to use but also that there is a plan to guard students from outside intrusion.

Discipline is an important part of classroom management. Disciplinary actions should promote a continuous effect of good behavior. Rules should be consistent, not only in a single classroom but throughout the school or district as well.

We believe one has to look at classroom management as having two components that must work together to attain success: planning and leading. If good plans are set in motion by effective, respected role models, measures of discipline should be kept to a minimum. The definition of accepted discipline changes from generation to generation. Accepted behavior changes less often. Expectations should remain barely unchanged, with the possible exception of constantly raising the bar for excellence.

Gathering and identifying scores of players is a fruitless effort unless there is also a good plan that is put into motion. As we discuss the individuals involved in making classroom management a success, we will examine the tools and skills needed to create our plans as well as several plans that have proven their success in schools around the world. Furthermore, we will illustrate the role of administrators and how they aid teachers in the proper selection and implementation of classroom management programs. We will see how these actions will result in raising and maintaining high test scores in a workplace that is enjoyed by both the faculty and students.

Before delving into this work, we must first dispel the often mistaken notion that new teachers are the only ones who would benefit from workshops, discussions, or courses on classroom management. One of the essential keys to successful leadership is continued self-growth. It is true that staff new to education will need guidance as they learn how to run their classrooms. However, there is one important factor we must not overlook.

Regardless of how long a person has been in his or her job, there is always someone somewhere who has come up with new ideas that should be shared. Seasoned veterans are the individuals who will act as mentors to new teachers. In order to provide proper and up-to-date information, these veterans need to remain current by regularly attending idea-sharing in-services, conferences, and workshops.

In the context of self-growth, a supervisor must account for his or her leadership by offering sound advice and by understanding and monitoring the faculty. Clinical supervision might be part of the answer. In his book *Leadership for Learning* (2002), Carl D. Glickman offers the following structure, which includes five sequential steps:

1. Preconference with teacher
2. Observation of classroom instruction
3. Analysis and interpretation of the observation and determination of the conference approach
4. Postconference with teacher
5. Critique of previous four steps

The leader might also consider "peer coaching," or mentoring, as some districts call it, as a formative technique in helping the teacher maintain a balance of control in the classroom. Self-growth on the part of the teacher would then be an expectation to seek out aid from colleagues and others in supervisory roles and to an extent self-reflection regarding doing things differently.

It is also essential that as leaders we exhibit strong, positive interpersonal skills while modeling the concepts and building our plan for good classroom management.

To that end, let us look at what both the students and the leaders expect from their schools. How do these expectations affect our general classroom management program? We have, surprisingly, found little in the way of research that illustrates the students' expectations of their school experience. This leads us to wonder that if we knew a bit more about what students were looking for, perhaps we might have an easier task when creating our classroom management plans.

Interestingly enough, even without sufficient data, as school leaders we tend to operate under the assumption that if a child is bored, or more social than his or her classmates, the result is a failed classroom management program. Our suggestion here would be to conduct a survey of educators, parents, and students to determine the exact expectations of each group. Only then, using this information as a guideline, can a successful program be formulated. The result should be a learning atmosphere where classroom management is a positive tool, not a chore or a fruitless effort.

Children, even more so than adults, are constantly seeking the approval of others. Students require the attention and acceptance of their parents, their educators, and their peers. An inability to connect, even if only as a perception on the part of the student, ultimately results in undesirable behavior on the part of the student. Classroom management programs will be ineffective. Therefore, knowing the students' expectations is not enough. A good classroom management program ensures that steps are taken to meet these expectations without compromising the integrity of the academic goals of your classroom, school, or district.

How do we combat this type of misbehavior, and in effect how can leaders help teachers with this dilemma? Some schools have adopted plans to bring students and teachers closer on a personal level to break down some of the barriers between them. Although varying degrees of these plans have been used, the goal is to build trust and foster a feeling of family. The theory is that if a student knows the teacher a bit more than by mere visual recognition, that student will react more positively when with that adult. This positive action/reaction makes classroom management an easier objective to obtain.

Unsuccessful classroom management plans result in unsuccessful, ineffective, and often disillusioned educators. People in these situations are more apt to leave their place of employment and seek better environs. The number of educators who do not last more than five years is arguably unacceptably high.

Richard Ingersoll (2002), of the University of Pennsylvania, stated that the fact that by the end of five years only 61 percent of teachers will still be in place confirms increases in both student numbers and teacher retirements. He found that the dominant factors contributing to these statistics include issues with student discipline and student motivation.

One means to invite new educators to remain on the job is to ensure that they enjoy and are successful in their positions. Ensuring that there is a desirable environment also helps to minimize the number of superintendent hearings or disciplinary actions. These factors together help maintain an overall good climate of the school or district, thereby providing an atmosphere that is pleasing to work in.

Chaos and lack of direction too often turn away potentially promising staff. Elimination of chaos and conversely the promotion of positive, clear direction can decrease the high rate of turnover for educators of all levels. Positive steps must be taken because only successful employees are apt to be content in their positions and less likely to look for an early career change.

Finally, as leaders we must not lose sight of the fact that new staff members are just that—new. They should not be expected to walk into a classroom, armed only with knowledge they gleaned in college, and be instantly successful.

What they do need is a role model to follow and a clearly defined message from their administrators on what is expected of them. The message should come from not only the administration but also the entire staff. If the classroom management plan is properly implemented, the new staff member can see evidence of the plan in the actions of the entire school community.

One must keep in mind that while teachers, new and veteran alike, are looking to their administrators to be decisive, strong leaders, they are also looking for the human side of those leaders. People are more apt to remain at their job sites if their supervisors respect them, acknowledge their strengths, and in the case of educators, view their teachers as intellectual professionals rather than specialized technicians.

Some schools have strict, distinct dividing lines that separate the level of social contact between teachers and administrators. Others have a relaxed, family-like atmosphere. Each school must decide, based on the dynamics of their particular situation, which direction to lean.

However, one must never lose sight of the fact that a climate of trust and understanding among the staff filters down to a climate of trust and understanding that includes the students. How one might expect to attain respect and ensure a successful management program depends on the characteristics and actions of the leaders.

As previously mentioned, the five essential skills that one must possess in order to be a successful school leader are keeping in touch with the community; exercising strong, positive interpersonal skills; being flexible; being insightful; and cultivating self-growth (Langley & Jacobs, 2006). Employing these skills on a regular basis ensures a successful classroom management program.

As we get started putting together our plan for a solid classroom management program, we must try to predict what types of situations might arise in our area. Next we must examine ways to prevent possible undesirable situations. Once we have done this, the roles of students, teachers, and administrators must be defined.

Administrators should lead, lend support, and be the final decision makers while not taking on the role of dictator. Teachers should be able to develop positive attributes in their students so that the students tend to contribute to the positive classroom management program. If student expectations are clearly defined and modeled, the ambiguity is removed and students begin to behave—and therefore learn—in the manner that is expected of them. Once the learning process becomes the focus, the potential for conflict as a means to resolve issues is diminished.

All too often, minor issues unnecessarily evolve into situations where fingers are pointed and little is resolved. Parents blame teachers and teachers blame administrators for lack of support in turning the tide of bad behavior in a classroom to an atmosphere of positive learning.

Therefore, it is crucial to explore methods in which the entire educational community can improve their classroom management programs. One must always remember that our objective is for the effective delivery of the daily lesson. Teachers cannot accomplish this without the support and aid of students, parents, and both the school-based and district-level administrators.

The majority of material we encountered pertaining to classroom management addresses the topic as a discipline issue above all else. With this in mind, we set forth in this book to illustrate how the focus on discipline is perhaps the least effective and not the sole component of a good classroom management program.

We contend that classroom management is not merely a method of discipline. It is a well-rounded program that promotes high academic achievement and a motivated learning environment. Through a specific classroom management program, with the aid of administrators and parents, all students benefit and will enjoy entering that classroom teacher's door.

THE ROLE OF TEACHERS

Although a good classroom management plan has many components, perhaps the most important we should keep in mind is that timing is of the essence. Parents, administrators, and teachers must begin communication with students before the first day of school. Well-planned orientation programs familiarize the parents with the school programs and expectations as well as provide students with the knowledge they need to enter into a successful school year.

On the first day of school, teachers should carefully explain their expectations to their students. To avoid confusion, individual expectations should not be in conflict with the overall school plan. Students are more apt to accept and follow rules if they are clear about what is expected of them. Dialogues between teachers and students to review plans help ease this process.

Furthermore, teachers should demonstrate a willingness to be flexible by listening to student concerns and a willingness to come to consensus regarding classroom rules or procedures that include input from the students. Once more, this is an issue that should be addressed during the first week of school lest habits that are difficult to break begin to take form.

Teachers should not hesitate to let kids talk—involve them and let them be part of the decision-making process. No matter how small of a role, as long as they take part, taking ownership helps build pride and leads to cooperative behavior.

Before delving into specific management techniques and administrative support, one should revisit the works of experts such as Vygotsky and Bloom regarding the socialization and various learning techniques of children (see, e.g., Bloom, 1976, 1981; Vygotsky & Cole, 1978). How and why are students social creatures? How do they learn?

Understanding how to deal with discipline problems and what administrators might consider is the key to creating effective management techniques. This helps the teacher have better classroom control so that effective and enthusiastic learning takes place.

Another characteristic of a successful teacher is that it is his responsibility to motivate others to follow the same path. A teacher should demonstrate that the benefits to be gained by being open-minded outweigh the minor inconvenience it takes to embrace other ideas.

Beginning with the first day, and followed by every school day, teachers should be present in the doorways to welcome students as they enter the classroom. Students should be addressed by name so as to build a feeling of confidence. On the same token, administrators should be present at the main entrance, around the hallways, and on the school grounds, and they should be ready to greet students, preferably by name.

Teacher techniques include everything in a teacher's bag of tricks, from the delivery of instruction of the actual curriculum to best practices/methods to the layout of the classroom/school. Popular theory is that when students become active participants in their learning experience, take ownership in what they are learning, and find relevance in their studies, they are more likely to stay on task and present less of a discipline problem. Studies dating as far back as the days of Marcus Fabius Quintilian (ca. A.D. 35 to ca.

A.D. 100) and working their way up to B. F. Skinner argue that positive and productive behavior on the part of students is a key motivation factor.

University classes teach our future educators that it is very important to begin instruction as soon as the students arrive in class by using warm-up activities. Warm-up exercises should provide an opportunity for students to interact with other students as well as with the material. Engaging students and allowing them to talk over what is being taught not only refreshes their memory from the previous lesson but also sets the tone for the business of learning. The goal is to keep students on task so that the delivery of the lesson is uninterrupted or that interruptions are kept to a minimum.

As we deliver our lessons, we must make certain that we try to acknowledge as many students as possible. While this may not seem an easy task in large classes, there are a few actions we can take to include everyone in the learning process. For example, when you pose a question to the class, give time for students to contemplate the possible answer, then call upon someone who was not the first to raise their hand. This provides the more quiet or shy students time to gain recognition.

Administrators play a major role here as they take measures to ensure that teachers have good, solid lesson plans. An administrator might suggest that teachers review their delivery of instruction so that the entire class is engaged at the same time. For example, a teacher might be assigning a project and devoting her attention to parts of the class while those not ready to engage must sit and wait their turn. A wait of even two minutes can spark enough distraction on the part of the waiting group to throw them completely off task, making it rather difficult for the teacher to regain the students' focus.

Mentor programs, for both new teachers and veteran teachers who are new to a particular school, work well. When possible, the mentor should be a teacher of the same subject as the new person. The mentor process should begin with an initial meeting before the rest of the staff arrives at the beginning of the school year. Present at this initial meeting should be the program leader, the mentors, all of the new teachers, and the entire administrative staff.

For optimum success, mentors should meet with their assigned new staff member at least twice per week. The program leader should set up monthly meetings where old and new business can be explained or reviewed. At least one administrator should be present at these monthly meetings.

It is up to the administrators to find workshops for their staff that address issues of classroom management, best practices, instructional overlap, and disciplinary procedures. Once identified, administrators must suggest that their staff attend at least a few. However, mere suggestion is not enough. Some accommodation has to be met. Funds should be earmarked to cover staff development workshops, substitute teacher coverage, and common planning time.

We must not overlook veteran teachers who may have been at the same school for years. Professionals, regardless of their area of expertise, do tend to fall into a rut wherein they begin to do their jobs by rote and not with the creativity and zeal of their first few years on the job. Teachers are no exception to this phenomenon. Teachers as well as administrators must keep alert to signs that they or their colleagues might have lost the effect they once had on their students. Signs to look for include the following:

- Generally lower student achievement in this class than is common for others in the same department
- A higher rate of disciplinary measures taken than the norm for the department, school, or individual student in question
- Inability to work well with parents; unusual amount of complaints from parents
- Lack of communication with parents
- Classrooms that seem chaotic or lack direction
- Classrooms where the students appear to be working out of fear rather than willingness to perform

- Excessive tardiness or absence of the teacher
- Unwillingness on the teacher's part to become involved in any extracurricular activities
- General lack of camaraderie with colleagues
- Overall aura of negativity

Finally, it is the responsibility of both teacher-colleagues and administrative staff to identify and assist individuals who have fallen into this phenomenon of being in a rut. Once identified, they must try to rectify the situation by coaching or mentoring via positive reinforcement to attain a learning environment that is pleasant and successful for both teacher and student. We must not forget self-evaluation, either. Teachers might videotape some of their class sessions and review the tape, alone or with a colleague, to determine the areas they themselves might improve upon.

A most valuable tool for self-assessment, as well as all components of a successful classroom management plan, is that of the professional learning community (PLC) defined and presented by Richard DuFour and Robert Eaker. PLCs provide a successful venue for teachers and administrators to review curriculum, delivery of instruction, and classroom management practices. Attendees to regularly scheduled PLC meetings could select their best lesson strategy or management actions to share with the rest of the staff. Equally as important, lesson plans or classroom management techniques that did not result in the desired goal should also be brought to the table.

Both success stories and failed attempts provide great learning tools that can be shared and discussed. Everyone in the PLC can adopt from the success stories. Things that did not work can be reviewed, and the group can work toward a mutual solution. While it is logical to include all faculty members in the PLC group, we must not omit school support staff, parents, and certain representatives of the local community. Involvement of parents and community will be addressed in upcoming chapters.

Personal conversation and observations play one part in the overall role of good classroom management. However, one must not overlook the importance of the atmosphere of the room, school building, surrounding grounds, and entire school. How often do we step back and consider these points when examining our classroom management plans?

Every classroom is designed a little differently from others. However, with few exceptions, they all have doors, windows, and walls. Proper arrangement of furniture and furnishings can contribute greatly to or detract from a classroom management program. We often notice that in two classrooms of the same size and shape, in the same school, the students who learn in both rooms do not behave the same in each. Perhaps one is orderly, where the children are busy, and there is a hum of activity. Conversely, in the other room, children are running and fighting over materials, and the noise level is disruptive for everyone. We have to ask ourselves what is different in each room that causes students to behave as such.

Does the time of day have a role? Yes, sometimes. Does the presence or absence of one or two particular students produce differing behavior of the whole group? Again, yes, perhaps it does—sometimes. One can only deduce that the teaching styles of the educators in each of the rooms are so different that it is the answer we are looking for. Perhaps, but what if their styles are similar? What we are left with is the physical layout of the room.

Classrooms that are designed in an efficient manner are conducive to reducing activities that are disruptive or undesirable. Certain subjects, such as science labs or physical education, would prevent us from providing a classroom setting that offers sofas, study tables, flowers in a vase, curtains on the windows, and so on. However, without taking redecorating to an extreme, we can arrange a classroom to be totally functional and efficient while not distracting from its aesthetic value. Nor will we have to seek funds to rebuild.

Before looking at the classroom setting, an area that is normally left to the creativity of the teacher, we should address the issue of the school building and grounds. Maintaining a clean environment, and including student involvement in doing so, helps instill the feeling of ownership and pride that is needed to gain the respect and interest of the students. Simple things such as having science classes work in any garden areas around the building—doing planting, weeding, minor landscaping—not only teach the children to work together but also provide a life skill while building a sense of ownership and pride. Wood-shop classes can lend a hand by constructing such items as flower boxes, landscaping borders, or other components of the outside areas around the school.

When students must leave the main building to attend classes in portable buildings, the condition of their paths has influence on their assessment of the overall environment. A clean perimeter, free of unnecessary obstacles, is viewed with more respect than a cluttered, unkempt area. A building that has too much of a neglected environment—overgrown or empty gardens, trash around the school yard, graffiti, broken windows or fences—does nothing to motivate students.

If a school has the appearance of an institution that is serious about learning, students are more likely to treat the school, and therefore each other, with respect and pride. Respect and pride are arguably the keys one might find in a model learning environment with a successful classroom management plan in action.

Another way to build esteem in students, adding to their sense of pride and ownership, is to provide them with a venue to brag. Bulletin boards and walls that demonstrate student work help encourage and motivate student achievement.

The physical arrangement of furniture and materials should create a positive atmosphere, thereby improving the overall climate of education. How a teacher designs and arranges his classroom may indicate to children how the room is to be used. Consideration should be made for even the smallest of items in the room. No matter the size or shape of a classroom, certain things can improve a classroom management program.

Placement of pencil sharpeners. If the pencil sharpener in a classroom is mounted in a location that is heavily trafficked during a lesson, a student who gets up to sharpen her pencil can create a distraction. For example, if the sharpener is on the wall in the front of a room, regardless of whether it is a college lecture hall or an elementary school classroom, a student needing to use the tool has to cross a path dividing the teacher from the students. All eyes, which until that point were on the teacher, board, or overhead, now turn to watch the wandering student. The train of concentration is broken. Student focus is misdirected. Getting some students back on task can be difficult. Therefore, one must look for an unobtrusive location—perhaps one that is either in the back of the room or by the doorway.

If the classroom is in an outdoor facility, such as a modular unit, a pencil sharpener on a common wall can create undue noise in the adjoining classroom. A simple step such as moving the sharpener to a wall that does not separate classes greatly reduces the noise created in the other room, thereby not disturbing student concentration.

Location of the sharpener should also be in a spot that allows free flow of students who wish to use it. A large gathering of students waiting in line, or in a mob, feeds students more fuel for distractions—such as conversations—that take a thirty-second task and turn it into a two-minute event. Additionally, the gathering of students around the sharpener will interrupt the teacher's ability to make contact with as many students as possible.

Clocks. The clock on the wall of a classroom can be the most distracting device in the room. Students, particularly at the secondary levels, have a keen sense of time and often seek out the clock to help them gauge how long they have until freedom. If a room is designed so that the wall clock is behind the students, two things can be accomplished.

First, the temptation to be a clock-watcher is reduced by the sheer discomfort of having to turn in one's seat. Second, a teacher becomes aware if a student has tuned out by noticing how frequently that student turns to see the clock. By noticing this behavior, the teacher can adjust her lesson accordingly to bring the student back on task. The role of the principal here is to support the teacher in her request to the custodial staff to position the clock in a desirable place.

Trash receptacles. While being a necessity for every room, trash receptacles that are not strategically placed only invite classroom management problems. If the receptacles are in an area that is heavily trafficked, students going to retrieve art paper from the back closet may create a traffic jam. A wastebasket quickly becomes a basketball hoop if placed where it tempts students to turn focus away from teachers and accept the challenge of a free throw.

Placing trash bins in the back of the classroom or by the door allows students to use them on the way in or out of the room. If the trash bins are by the pencil sharpener, a student who simply must clear away unwanted trash during the lesson can do so by accomplishing two tasks at once. Students might also be instructed that if they have trash to deposit they might take it with them as they exit the room to use the restroom, go to the clinic, or attend whatever issue might call them out of class.

Desk arrangement. The age level of the students often dictates classroom arrangement. Fred Jones suggests that teachers at the elementary level may wish to situate furniture so that it separates work areas from activity areas. In a sense, such configurations create obstacles that deter children from running through the classroom. However, similar settings would also be well suited for older students, such as high school aged, for large classes (thirty or more students), and for subjects where students might not be out of their seats often. For example, a separated setting, or one made of small groupings with all students facing the front of the room, would work for lectures, study halls, literature, government, and so on.

For middle or high schools, an arrangement with plenty of room for the teacher to easily visit each desk is best for classes with a lot of group work such as the sciences, a publication or journalism class, yearbook, or any other class where the diversity of the student population is such that students benefit from cooperative learning activities. This type of arrangement also provides for heterogeneous grouping so that stronger students might help peers who are struggling with the class.

However, there are times, particularly in secondary schools, when it might be beneficial to arrange furniture so that there is a constant large area of open space. Most rooms allow for some variation of a "U," or horseshoe, type of arrangement. By doing so, the room provides a fair amount of open space that would be most conducive to such activities as student skit performances in classes such as foreign languages, drama, social studies, or language arts classes. A semi-horseshoe inside another semi-horseshoe, with an opening in the back of the room, allows a flow of traffic for students and easy access for the teacher. Regardless of grade level, the furniture should be arranged so that it ensures that the teacher is always located where he has an "eye" on all class activities.

Student common areas, such as computer stations, reading areas, supply centers, and worktables, should be placed far enough away from the desk areas so as not to distract from lessons.

The role of the administrative staff is not one to be overlooked when it comes to classroom furniture. For example, if a principal is about to order new desks or chairs, he or she might want to poll the teachers first to find out what type of furniture might best suit the teaching styles of that site. We are not suggesting here that administrators try to work beyond their budgets to accommodate one teacher, but that a well-developed PLC would have input into the type of furniture that would benefit the school as a whole.

When looking at the design or layout of a classroom, we must not overlook the area directly outside the doorway. Often class time is disrupted while teachers wait for students to take out and turn in homework. Perhaps the class is further disrupted by students getting up and delivering homework to a specified location.

If all students do not enter the room with homework in hand, this can take up valuable learning minutes. On the same lines, if a teacher has a special notice or work to be handed out to students, doing this during class time again detracts from lesson time. A simple classroom management tool that can easily be learned by students—particularly if it is put into place the first days of the school year—is to leave a well-placed receptacle near the door.

General distractions. The overall atmosphere of the school site, inside and out, contributes to the attitude of students and faculty alike. A positive area that promotes a safe and pleasant learning environment affects the success of classroom management. Therefore, the next focus should be on the school as a whole.

Building facility committees must take several things into consideration, beyond structural or financial concerns. Placement of such items as windows, doors, and storage areas has great impact on overall classroom management. When installing chalkboards in new or renovated classrooms, for example, they should be, whenever possible, positioned in such a manner that the focus of attention for the class as a whole is toward the board, with the windows behind the students. Windows offer a wonderful view of our natural surroundings, but they can interfere with the learning process.

Locker bay areas should be designed to allow for a free flow of traffic. Lockers need to be large enough to accommodate books, backpacks, and personal items. However, the height of lockers in freestanding bay areas can play an important role in overall classroom management. Lockers that are taller than students impede the ability of teachers who are monitoring hall activity to clearly spot students who are avoiding moving on to their classes or who are engaging in inappropriate activities.

Cafeterias are a place where students have some time to relax and socialize. However, they must remember that they are expected to act as responsible students—as members of their school society. Rules in the cafeteria that promote responsibility carry into the classrooms, and conversely if student time in the cafeteria is a free-for-all, this attitude will follow students back into the hallways.

There are several plans that are quite effective for promoting cafeteria responsibility and overall classroom management. If students leave the cafeteria without cleaning their immediate surroundings, they develop a sense that they need not be responsible for their own actions. Teaching students to clean up after themselves, while working with their peers, instills in them a sense of responsibility as well as a sense of cooperation that they will soon grasp as routine.

Each and every student should not only be responsible for maintaining their own area, they should also learn to help each other. Duties can be divided on a daily or weekly schedule wherein some tables are responsible for cleaning off the tables while others are to sweep up the floor. Monitors can be assigned to the trash area and tray return area to assist in swift and efficient work.

The smaller the group, the easier it is to contain and to maintain order. Cafeteria tables should not be so large as to fit more than eight students. Tables where the seats are attached are ideal for subtly carrying out this idea. If bullying or fighting has been an issue, attached seating also reduces the continuation of such activities. Students cannot pull the seats out from others. Chairs cannot be used as weapons. Suspected gang members cannot all sit at one table, especially if there are more members than there are chairs.

Naturally, adult supervision is needed in the cafeteria to maintain order and to be present in the event of an emergency. While teachers are usually the designated adults for this activity, it is important that administrators be present for all lunch periods. Again, this presence sends a message to both students and teachers that the administrators are aware of what is going on in the school and more important that they care.

Finally, the practice of adult supervision in the cafeteria is one that can be extended to include community involvement and not just at the elementary level. Parent volunteers should be invited to participate in this activity. This arrangement not only shows students that parents care about their school life but also gives parents a better idea of the way a cafeteria operates in a school and teaches them a bit about the social practices of their children in an environment other than the classroom or home.

Schoolwide rules, routines, and schedules. Nothing is more destructive to an attempt to implement a plan than chaos. Schools should not be so rigid as to stifle creativity, nor should they be lacking any rules or semblance of order. Children of all ages rely on the guidance of others to help them, regardless of how independent a child wants one to think he is. In a school setting, children should receive a good amount of this guidance from the adult role models—teachers and administrators. An effective plan to encourage students to comply with regulations is one that provides a brief yet informative explanation as to why a specific rule was created.

It is imperative not to send children mixed messages. If one teacher ignores a rule, such as issuing consequences for being tardy, chewing gum, or violating dress-code guidelines, it sends a message to children that some people can interpret rules as they please. The same holds true for teachers or other staff members as role models. A student should not expect to be disciplined for wearing certain clothing deemed inappropriate in one classroom, by one teacher, if the school dress code does not prohibit such clothing. Nor should the rule be required of students if adults in the building violate the same codes.

Teachers, as well as administrators, must be in agreement regarding the deliverance of consequences. A student becomes unsure of how to behave if, for example, she is reprimanded by one teacher for shouting out answers without being called upon yet is not subject to face consequences from another teacher for the same offense.

One example of sending mixed messages to students comes from teachers who ignore the rules of the building. Releasing students early from classrooms is a universal concern among teachers. Ignoring this important rule not only causes disruption in the hallways but also interferes with the learning process of other classes still in session. In addition, having students in the hallways early without teacher supervision is a high-risk safety factor.

An invitation to break down an atmosphere of order occurs when individuals begin to make unilateral decisions. Rules must be uniform and not changed from one classroom to another. There must be agreement at school or grade level as to the rules and their subsequent consequences. The students must be fully acquainted with rules and consequences, and all staff members need to have a voice in forming rules and consequences for their school site.

Administrators should make certain that there is no ambiguity on the part of their staff as to what the rules are, and why. While realizing that it is important for students to learn to make choices, merely telling them that something is not permitted is not a solution. You have to provide examples. Once the adults are all aware of the rules, students must be brought on board.

Whereas an adult might be capable of learning a rule the first time it is explained and perhaps might benefit from a gentle reminding once, a child needs to be reminded many times over. Therefore, a system should be set in place that provides constant reminders, as well as proof of understanding on the part of the students. Simple, effective, and inexpensive reminders can blend into the routine, such as by placing arrows on stairwells to remind students which side to use to eliminate traffic jams. Not only do the students begin to follow these traffic patterns when the halls are crowded, but the ever-present indicators serve to remind students of what is expected of them, and they are more likely to adhere to these practices every time they use the stairwell.

Orderly behavior in the hallway is carried into the classroom as easily as chaos and disruption. If students migrate from class to class without feeling rushed or confused, the likelihood of their entering the classroom calmly and at ease is heightened, thereby making it easier for the teacher to run a successful lesson. Another means of easing tension in the hallways is to clearly post important information, such as the direction to take to locate specific rooms by posting maps or simple signs throughout the school.

When posting such information, it is important to take into consideration the general population of the school. Particular attention should be directed to the non-English speakers. High school students that we interviewed said that the signs they found themselves paying attention to were brightly colored, in large print, written in several languages, and strategically placed. Sometimes signs placed in areas that adults feel are the most logical might not be attention-getters for children. Our interviewees stated that the signs they notice most are those that are in places that one normally would not look for information, such as very low on a wall, on windows, by snack machines, in locker bays, or any place students hang around to chat with their friends.

Establishing, imposing, and distributing information on consequences. In addition to ensuring that everyone understands the rules, very clear-cut outlines must be set to institute a system of addressing the consequences for not following rules. For example, if a regulation states that a student may not arrive tardy to class, it must also provide a clear definition of tardy, a definitive consequence, and assurance from the administrators that there will be a follow-up on their part as set in the school's discipline guidelines or code of conduct.

Districtwide rules may not seem to fit at certain sites. Teachers, as well as school-based administrators, should not hesitate to discuss policy and regulations with the central administration and school board to gain a better understanding of such rules. However, when it comes to handbook regulations of the buildings, districtwide code of conduct policies, and districtwide regulations, all teachers and administrators should apply all such circumstances in a "one size fits all" manner to avoid legal issues and contractual obligations.

It is not uncommon to notice that in one school building, individual teachers handle consequences for tardies differently. This does nothing to help the student nor to support the PLC. While we might tend to believe that our jobs would be easier if we rely on the "one rule fits all" theory, in most circumstances—particularly when it comes to lateness or absenteeism—that rule does not apply. There are always extenuating and personal circumstances that might account for a tardy or an absence; however, it should not be up to the individual teacher to decide if or how to act. There must be a school policy that is strictly adhered to by all. To comply with legal requirements, the school must be able to accurately show documented accounting for a student's whereabouts during their entire school day. If a student arrives late to class, regardless of how a teacher might view the tardiness, it must be made part of the official record. Consequences for being tardy or having excessive absences can be dealt with on an individual basis, but reporting these actions must be consistent. Each teacher should adhere to the blanket school policy by reporting lateness and absenteeism. Administrators in these cases can help the teacher or staff member by applying that consequence in an equality perspective or at the very least, in an equity sense. This ensures that a teacher reporting the incident to the appropriate building administrator does follow up and gives the staff the feeling that their initiatives are supported.

Most any actions that exercise some sort of discipline as a means to accomplish a goal can lead to an undesirable outcome. Therefore, when considering disciplinary action, one must take care to follow the lead of our judicial system in which expectations and consequences for not adhering to rules are clearly defined. In addition, those people affected—particularly students—must be made aware of these expectations and consequences, not unlike the Miranda ruling used by our police and courts.

Administrative support to enhance teacher management skills. There are many ways an administrator can show his support for the classroom teacher. One such way involves the interaction of teachers and parents. Administrators should be aware of the type of relationship between both parties. To this end, teachers should keep accurate records of phone calls, e-mails, and personal contact with parents. There may be times when the administrator deems it necessary to sit in on a personal meeting, but generally this decision should be left to the teachers.

At parent–teacher meetings, administrators should show impartiality yet support for the teacher. If there is a matter in which the administrator does not agree with the teacher's position, conversation about this should take place before the arrival of the parent if possible. If not, the administrator should refrain from admonishing or disagreeing with the teacher in the presence of the parent and address the issue after the meeting ends and the parent is not present.

At a meeting with a parent, the administrator should demonstrate support for the teacher yet be a strong mediator who can suggest compromises that would satisfy all parties without straying from school or district policy. For example, if a parent–teacher conference is held because of the student's misbehavior, it is the responsibility of the administrator to explain the code of conduct to the parent and then facilitate an agreed-upon consequence that is in accordance with policy and accepted by parent, teacher, and administrator. This ensures that the parent is well informed of the expectations of the student and hopefully demonstrates that the actions of the teacher were in concert with this policy.

In order for this to be a successful effort, it is the responsibility of the administrator to ensure that the teachers are fully familiar with the conduct policy. Monthly faculty meetings provide a wonderful venue in which teachers and administrators can review these and other essential policies. An effective administrator uses her positive, strong interpersonal skills (Langley & Jacobs, 2006) to bring the entire staff to the same wavelength.

Should a meeting turn to heightened emotions between parent and teacher, it is the responsibility of the administrator to act as a buffer and direct the meeting to one where the issues can be calmly addressed. At all times, the topic of the meeting should remain focused and not be permitted to stray off target. Again, it might be the role of the administrator to ensure that this is done. Impartiality is essential and includes not only the action/reaction of the teacher and parent but also should never lead the meeting to a point where fingers are pointed at the student as the sole or main reason for the meeting.

While on the surface it might seem as such, the teachers and administrators must not alienate the parent and therefore must come up with solutions that indicate a willingness for the school personnel to work with the parent and student to resolve the issue. In a review from the Internet site of Education World Principal Files, Tracy Berry-Lazo (2003) concluded that "educators who feel the problem is the kids, and that they have no influence over their students' behaviors, might want to consider writing books instead of entering the classroom."

Equally as important as it is to make certain that the teachers are aware of policy, we must make sure that students know objectives and expectations in the classroom and in the school. To maintain good classroom management, these objectives have to be kept constant, and a strong program of character education will go a long way in assisting a school to keep students apprised of the expectations placed upon them.

Let us examine the plight of a new student to middle school and the few simple actions that may have negative results that could be easily nipped in the bud. The main character in our story, "Ricky," is a compilation of students we have all encountered in our school experiences. Our fictional student is entering middle school for the first time and faces difficult situations with his peers, teachers, and administrators. The issues Ricky faces are ones that allow us to demonstrate specific management techniques that improve not only classroom behavior of students but the overall academic environment.

Ricky was a model elementary school student both academically and artistically. The other students looked to him as a leader. His teachers often praised his work and work habits. Sixth grade was over, and now Ricky was about to enter middle school. He was a little unsure of himself for the first time in his young life. Over the summer he drifted from some of his old classmates, and he began to withdraw a bit, preferring to engage in activities that did not require interaction with other children. His parents did not take much notice of this and attributed what they did see to the fact that most of Ricky's friends went away for parts of the summer, and he did not.

During the orientation program for the new seventh-grade students, Ricky was thrilled to see his old friends but was taken aback at the sight of all the new faces from the other elementary schools that fed into his new school. He was made more ill at ease when a quick comparison of their class schedules indicated that his closest friends were not in the majority of his classes. Most were not even on his grade-level team.

The morning of the first day of school, when the alarm went off, Ricky was too tired to get out of bed, and his mom inadvertently allowed him to oversleep. Ricky seemed fine, but he uncharacteristically lagged behind. His mom told him that he'd best be ready for school when she returned from driving his younger siblings to elementary school.

They finally arrived at school and found that Ricky had missed the first class and was late for the second. When he entered into second period, the teacher was so far into explaining the course that she did not have time to let him introduce himself to the others. In fact, the teacher was a bit annoyed that Ricky disrupted her agenda, and she allowed her disappointment to show.

As Ricky took his seat, some of his former classmates made a big issue of greeting him, further interrupting the teacher and further raising her anxiety. Ricky knew he did not start this class on the right foot and was certain the new teacher would hold his interruption against him all year. Unfortunately, later that day, at the first team meeting, this teacher was quick to point out that she thought Ricky should be red-flagged as a potential discipline problem.

Feeling rather lost and alone, Ricky was relieved to finally enter the cafeteria for lunch. The principal and the two assistant principals provided cafeteria supervision the first week of school. By the time Ricky entered the seating area, the only available table was with a group of eighth-grade boys whom Ricky recognized as a bunch that he was often warned by his parents to steer clear of. They often caused problems around the neighborhood and were familiar to the local police.

One of the assistant principals walked over to talk with the boys. He thought Ricky was the newest member of the group that gave the school the most trouble the previous year. He welcomed the boys and reminded them that their actions would be closely watched again this year. As he turned to speak with Ricky, he was called away by the other administrator. Now Ricky realized he was guilty by association and missed his only opportunity to explain that he was not part of the group.

On the bus ride home, the driver was not in the best of spirits. She did not know Ricky's face since he did not ride to school on the bus that morning, and when she questioned him, Ricky mistook her sullen attitude as yet another force against him at the end of a horrible day and uncharacteristically rudely answered back. This caused the driver to react by making Ricky sit in the front seat, directly under her watchful eye.

Naturally, Ricky's lunch buddies took in all the fuss and immediately labeled Ricky as a potential new addition to their crowd. Finally, as the bus pulled up to Ricky's house, his mom was in the driveway and got a full report from the bus driver. His mom was shocked; she had never received such a report about Ricky. She told him to go to his room and that they'd deal with it after she got the younger siblings settled. Of course, she got busy and quickly forgot all about the incident.

Meanwhile, Ricky went to his room and went over the events of the day. He was doomed. The die had been cast. His old friends were busy making new friends, and the guys who seemed to take to him were exactly the kind of boys he avoided until now. He was scared in his new environment and felt as though everything was going against him personally. After only one day in middle school, Ricky knew his life was about to change—and not for the better!

The questions we must seek to resolve are not as difficult as they may appear at first glance. However, nor do they come with quick, simple solutions. We can take two approaches to examine Ricky's hypothetical yet realistic problem. First, how could all of this been eliminated before it was allowed to take hold?

Next, we might explore how to look toward day two and how the immediate future might affect the rest of Ricky's career as a student. What should happen now to reach Ricky before he makes the wrong choices? In taking this approach, we have to determine how each of the characters in Ricky's life must work together to steer Ricky along the right path. Who should be held responsible for the actions that took place? We might explore how to put in motion a plan that would work toward avoiding situations such as the one Ricky now faces. Who should be responsible for rectifying the situation to avoid future plights like this one?

Providing a smooth and friendly transition from elementary school to middle school would be the first step in avoiding Ricky's plight. The middle school should offer an orientation program that allows students to

- get acquainted with the new building,
- meet the counselors and teachers,
- see students in action—perhaps by looking in on some of the classes in session,
- hear/see performances by the music, drama, and art departments,
- learn about club and athletic opportunities,
- become familiar with using lockers, and
- meet students from other feeder elementary schools.

It is not the sole responsibility of the school or schools to ensure a smooth transition from one level to another. The parent has a definite role in this situation. We address this matter in depth in chapter 3. However, for now let us look at Ricky's situation and try to determine what role his parents, particularly in this case, his mother, should have played. First, we note that Ricky's mom should have been aware of the sudden change in his attitude as the day drew nearer when Ricky would have to leave his comfortable routine and enter the new world of middle school.

She might have noticed that he was a bit unsure of himself, that he was uncharacteristically withdrawn, and that his withdrawal was in fact a signal that he needed a friendly face. If his parents were accustomed to family dinners together, perhaps it would have come out in discussion that Ricky was harboring some fears and doubts about going to his new school. Noticing that most of his friends went away for the summer, perhaps they might have approached one of the other parents to see if it would have been okay to send Ricky along with them.

If the mom had taken a few minutes to enquire about Ricky's experience at the orientation, she would have learned that he was concerned about all of the changes that he felt ill-prepared to face. Therefore, she could have either calmed his fears by discussing them with him, or she might have taken him to meet with the counselors to let them work on easing the transition. The school might not have set up a clearly marked area where teachers and counselors could meet the new students and their parents in order to answer any pressing questions they might have.

The fact that Ricky was uncharacteristically late getting out of bed on the first day of school should have been the final red flag to indicate to his mom that something was not right. Although at that point it was rather late to allay his fears, his mom still had time to sit and chat with Ricky to find out what was wrong. A little assurance that she would be there upon his return in the afternoon to discuss his first day might have been the little comfort Ricky sought. Perhaps she might have told him of a situation she faced when she was his age that put her in an awkward position and then demonstrated for him how she survived the ordeal.

Because of the demands placed on parents due to their busy work schedules or other family duties, oftentimes little red flags such as the ones exhibited by Ricky up to and including his first day go unnoticed by even the most caring parents. It is important that parents realize that the first day of school can be like the first day on a new job. Students, like adults, need a comforting smile or an ear to listen to help calm the first-day jitters. Schools might remind parents of this transition period for students in the welcome letters that are sent home before the opening of each school year.

It was a bit unfair on Ricky's part to assume that the teacher from second period would have a negative attitude toward him for the entire year based on one bad first impression. However, his assumption was based on the reaction of the teacher when he entered the room late. Her inability to mask her disappointment did nothing to change his opinion. The teacher has the responsibility of conveying the message to all students that they are partners in the education process and that they are allowed to take risks. Risk takers are valued, and students should be made aware that mistakes could be used as learning opportunities.

On day two, the teacher should allow Ricky to catch up on what he missed the first day: take a few seconds to allow him to introduce himself to the class, let his new classmates introduce themselves, make certain that Ricky receives any handouts he missed on day one, and welcome him to the class.

The administrators who first encountered Ricky in the cafeteria need to revisit Ricky to determine whether he is in fact part of the difficult students before labeling him as such. The administrators had previous experience with the other boys at the table, but this was their first encounter with Ricky.

An administrator who properly uses his ability to be insightful (Langley & Jacobs, 2006) does not use one brief encounter to automatically assess a situation. Before labeling Ricky as one of the students who need to be under a watchful eye, the administrator must assess the situation and then make a more informed opinion of Ricky's potential.

The administrators might steer Ricky to new middle school opportunities in which he might demonstrate the strong academic and artistic abilities that we saw in Ricky the elementary school student.

Perhaps the administrators could introduce Ricky to the teacher-sponsor of the math club or yearbook committee. This would not only make middle school more appealing to Ricky but might also ensure that we guide him down the right path toward a successful education career.

The situation regarding Ricky, although touching on many points of classroom management, reveals only a small sampling of situations that might occur in a school on any given day. In order to provide a safe and positive learning environment, there are some practices that all teachers and administrators should follow. We devote the rest of this book to discussing particular methods that create a better environment for students such as Ricky.

Of course, there are no programs that ensure that all children behave as model students and grow up to be pillars of the community. As much as we would like to live in a perfect society, unfortunately, Utopia exists only in a fantasy world. Therefore, while facing reality we must ask ourselves what tools we have in our real world that we can use to reduce the number of problems and offer our students an optimum, well-rounded education, in and out of the schoolhouse.

Issues of education do not start and end with textbooks. Education is not confined to the classroom. The level of academic proficiency is not the only tool we use to measure student success. What measures could the local schools employ to help ensure that students become a positive contributor to society?

An effective school plan includes instruction in the traditional subjects such as reading, math, and science but also includes subjects that help increase a student's creative ability and socially accepted behavior. The first part of this idea is accomplished through a wide variety of elective courses beginning at the elementary school age.

These courses can include learning a foreign language; art classes that include all mediums such as photography; hands-on skills such as wood shop, mechanics, computer sciences, and media communications; and music programs that go beyond traditional band and chorus.

Our school days are understandably filled with standard courses designed to help students meet the requirements of the standardized tests that determine the success and accreditation of our schools. Many of the nontraditional classes that are not accountable to benchmarks and standardized tests do not have to be offered during the course of a normal school day. If at all possible, funds should be identified to allow presentation of these activities after normal school hours.

Should the budget have absolutely no room to include after-hours salaries, it is up to the PLC to find a way to include the entire community to accomplish this task. Business partners, parents, and other volunteers from the community can provide the adult supervision and expertise to run such programs. The number of teachers or other faculty members could be kept to a bare minimum—perhaps one to oversee the program—thereby keeping costs as low as possible.

These programs would provide a wealth of knowledge for our students, and their continued presence in the school building and engagement in positive activities contribute to their ownership and sense of belonging to their school, thereby further facilitating the everyday classroom management task of the teachers and administrators.

Extracurricular activities have proven successful in directing children's efforts toward positive, productive behavior in both rural and inner-city schools. The many examples of the success of

after-school activities can be seen in programs such as those presented by Rafe Esquith of Los Angeles, winner of the American
Teacher Award, who opened his classroom from 6:30 a.m. until
5:00 p.m. to help students who needed and wanted that extra bit of
assistance; Jamie Escalante of *Stand and Deliver* fame, who gave
up his personal time and put his own health problems aside to
work with students to build on their academic achievement as well
as their self-confidence; Ron Clark, who moved from the rural
Southeast to an inner-city school in New York City and demonstrated how raising the bar can raise interest and academic success;
and Daniel Ponickly, who developed a dance program for fifth
graders in New York City.

These are only four of the many, many educators who have used
their creativity, demonstrated their dedication, and sacrificed their
personal time to motivate and bring success to their students' lives.
Thankfully there are many unsung heroes who go that extra mile,
who use their time wisely, and who exercise their creativity to the
maximum possibility.

Yet, try as we may, some students will not participate in programs
merely because they have been designed to help them. Others still
may participate but fall prey to outside influence and continue
down a path of undesirable deeds, winding up in detention halls or
dropping out of school completely. For these students, as well as for
the less problematic students who on occasion need discipline, a
discipline program must be well established and presented to faculty, students, parents, and the entire school community.

Creating a plan is but the tip of the iceberg. The success of the
plan can only be realized when the plan is enacted. No matter what
type of plan is formed, the entire school must be willing to accept
and enforce it. Students need to have a clear understanding of
what is expected of them. If they do not, we cannot reprimand
them for behavior that we do not favor. The time to deliver the
plan or expectations to students is in the very first week of the
school year. As the year progresses, perhaps each quarter, individ-

ual teachers as well as the administrative team should ensure that these rules are reviewed by parents, students, and faculty.

Once everyone is on board, there are two main ideas we must keep in mind. Consequences lose their meaning if they are not presented as soon as possible after the undesired action. The time between when a student performs an infraction of the school/ district code and the time he or she is confronted by an administrator should be swift, perhaps no more than twenty-four hours. If an incident goes unattended too long, the student is apt to forget why he or she is being punished, details of the incident begin to fade, and the overall success of remediation becomes lost.

The second point is that the punishment should match the crime, so to speak. A school program must clearly spell out consequences for each infraction, and the entire staff must follow them. For example, if a student knows that appearing late for one teacher's class will not result in any consequences, she is less likely to make every effort to arrive on time to all classes.

Well-disciplined children provide an atmosphere where it is easier for the teacher to get a point across without distraction. However, one would be wise to heed the teachings of B. F. Skinner and John Dewey, both subscribers to the idea that a successful school environment does not emulate an institution of authoritarian control. Students should be motivated, not coerced, to learn. Therefore, when developing a successful classroom management plan, careful detail should be devoted to the overall school atmosphere.

These men, among others, are advocates of an environment where learners are given freedom to develop creativity, but not by abandoning a system of control. Rather, control should be such that it produces positive results in a nonauthoritarian manner. In addition to making the rules clear, modeling expected behavior is essential.

For example, teachers cannot expect students to follow a dress code if the teachers do not. If the school rule is that cell phones are not permitted during class time, teachers ought not to have their phones engaged during a lesson.

As children learn and grow, expectations also grow. This increasing demand for responsibility and accountability can be a difficult adjustment for some children. A child's resentment of the increased demands and expectations can be misdirected toward the teachers who are giving the assignments.

Consequently, some children see their teachers as the villains responsible for their dissatisfaction, thereby allowing the children to view school as a place with which they would rather not associate. Naturally, this makes the task of students' accepting a classroom management plan all the more challenging. However, challenging does not mean impossible. Exercising the essential skills of a successful educator (Langley & Jacobs, 2006) facilitates the process.

Modeling expected behavior and overall classroom management on the part of the teacher is not confined to within the walls of the classroom. At class-change times, teachers should not only be present at the doorways but also alert to the goings-on in the halls. Often the mere presence of an adult is enough to deter a student from misbehaving in the hallways, but more often it is necessary for the teachers to be active participants.

Take a few steps away from the threshold and mingle at the outskirts of student groups. Not only will your presence make students think twice about their actions, but you are sure to gain insight to the students and their activities—positive as well as negative.

Observing hallway activity helps you learn the names of students who are not in your classes. When you notice unacceptable activity brewing, you can address the student or students involved by name. This fosters a bond, albeit a weak one, between you and the student. Students are apt to respond more positively to someone who knows them rather than a complete stranger.

Sending an uncontrollable student to stand in the hallway for any part of the class period is counterproductive. While your class might appear to run more smoothly without this student present, and the child may not have been taking full benefit of your class, in the hall he learns nothing of the lesson.

Conversely, the student may become a distraction to other classes and students while in the hall. A better way to handle such a situation would be to quietly let the child know that his behavior is not acceptable and that you will deal with it later. This interaction should take no more than fifteen seconds so as not to call attention to the disruptive child and further interrupt the learning process. While the student may feel a bit uncomfortable about being singled out, it will be much less than the humiliation caused by being sent to stand in the hallway as an outcast.

Brief, private conversation with a problem student is preferred to having that student face public condemnation by having her name written on the board to remind the whole class of an impending detention.

Dressing down a student in front of everyone serves only to alienate that student from you and make a bad situation worse. Just as you would not appreciate being admonished by your boss in front of colleagues, neither does a student appreciate being humiliated in front of peers.

We have come a long way from corporal punishment in our schools, and yet we still produce students who are highly educated and successful citizens. Practices in the past were often simple, direct, and uncomplicated, albeit illegal by today's standards. Regardless, they were also highly ineffective, not to mention arguably immoral.

The following is a true story of a student-teaching experience at a high school some thirty years ago in a relatively conservative town in the Midwest. As was the practice, some teaching took place, but organizing files, small-group instruction, and babysitting was the order of the day. Like other student teachers in that school, our student teacher was assigned to monitor a study hall.

To set the stage in this traditionalist arena, one must imagine walls that were free of any educational posters regarding learning, standards, and pictures of faraway places such as universities those students might attend after graduation. The room was stark; the armchair desks were aligned in straight rows and bolted to the floor. This particular study hall was true to the definitive word. Every last student in that room had his or her head bowed, reading carefully the books and homework assigned to them.

Since this was our student teacher's first placement, he thought that this was how things were done in the Midwest. Being from a large metropolis, he knew that this was not the norm in all high schools around the country. Suddenly, the silence was broken by a very loud crack. Startled, the student teacher immediately stood up, thinking that one of the chairs had given way, and looked for the fallen student. Not one student looked up from the obligatory assignment to see what caused the sound. Not one student so much as blinked.

After checking the room and feeling assured that the sound did not come from any broken chair, the student teacher asked the class if they knew what caused the disturbance. One student stated, just as a matter of fact, that the assistant principal was paddling a classmate.

In those days, paddling was the simple, direct, and uncomplicated method of discipline. There was a limited number of referral forms to fill out, no discussing the misbehavior with the school psychologist, no searching for past records on the student, no calling the parents first for their permission to discipline their child, and no punishment that seemed to interfere with legal issues and normal school operations.

At times we might feel a desire to resort to discipline in this archaic, ineffective method. However, while we believe that this type of classroom management might correct misbehavior, in fact our desire to revert to corporal punishment is merely a release mechanism of the frustration we have at that moment in time regarding the situation. But in acting as such, we again go back to being ineffective and surrounded by bolted armchair desks.

Although most educators agree that corporal punishment is not the desired action to take, to this day, there are districts that allow administrators to paddle a child up to and including the eighth grade. According to statistics from the United States Department of Education (USDOE), during the 1999–2000 school year, the total U.S. public school enrollment was 46,306,355. A study conducted by the USDOE Office for Civil Rights (2000) reported that 342,031 students nationwide were subjected to corporal punishment that one year alone.

While at first this may seem like a very high number, it is indeed a drop of 7 percent from the previous survey two years earlier, continuing a steady trend. Twenty-seven states and the District of Columbia prohibited all corporal punishment in public schools after the statistics were published. Data for the remaining twenty-three states at that time are demonstrated in table 1.1.

Table 1.1. **Incidents of Corporal Punishment in the United States**

State	Number of Students Hit	Percentage of Total Students
Alabama	39,197	5.4
Arizona	632	<0.1
Arkansas	40,437	9.1
Colorado	260	<0.1
Delaware	65	0.1
Florida	11,405	0.5
Georgia	25,189	1.8
Idaho	23	<0.1
Indiana	2,221	0.2
Kansas	99	<0.1
Kentucky	2,797	0.4
Louisiana	18,672	2.6
Mississippi	48,627	9.8
Missouri	9,223	1.0
New Mexico	2,205	0.7
North Carolina	5,717	0.5
Ohio	1,085	0.1
Oklahoma	17,764	2.9
Pennsylvania	407	<0.1
South Carolina	3,631	0.5
Tennessee	38,373	4.2
Texas	73,994	1.9
Wyoming	8	<0.1
U.S. Total	**342,031**	**0.7**

Source: U.S. Department of Education, Office for Civil Rights (2000)

During the 2004–2005 school year, according to the U.S. Department of Education, there was approximately an 11 percent drop in corporal punishment from the previously reported 1999–2000 school year number of students subjected to corporal punishment nationwide. Five states account for almost 73 percent of all corporal punishment incidents: Texas, Mississippi, Arkansas, Alabama, and Tennessee, and African American children receive more than 38 percent of all corporal punishment in the United States. See tables 1.2 and 1.3.

In New York State, the commissioner's regulations provide school districts with the power to adopt and implement a written policy on school conduct and discipline. The Schools Against Vio-

Table 1.2. Update of Incidents of Corporal Punishment in the United States

State	Number of Students Hit	Percentage of Total Students
Alabama	36,130	4.85
Arkansas	36,957	7.25
Arizona	1,583	0.16
Colorado	1	<.01
Florida	9,711	0.38
Georgia	19,826	1.29
Idaho	332	0.13
Indiana	2,737	0.26
Kansas	106	0.02
Kentucky	2,825	0.43
Louisiana	14,165	1.95
Missouri	4,371	0.48
Mississippi	40,692	8.01
North Carolina	2,718	0.19
New Mexico	722	0.21
Ohio	80	<.01
Oklahoma	12,715	2.04
*Pennsylvania	6	<.01
South Carolina	2,509	0.36
Tennessee	33,353	3.38
Texas	50,489	1.17
Wyoming	1	<.01

* PA banned in 05
Source: U.S. Department of Education, Office for Civil Rights (2000)

Table 1.3. The 10 Worst States, by Percentage of Students Struck by Educators in the 2003–2004 School Year

Rank	State	Percentage
1	Mississippi	8.0
2	Arkansas	7.3
3	Alabama	4.9
4	Tennessee	3.4
5	Oklahoma	2.0
6	Louisiana	2.0
7	Georgia	1.3
8	Texas	1.2
9	Missouri	0.5
10	Kentucky	0.4

Source: U.S. Department of Education, Office for Civil Rights (2000)

lence in Education Act (SAVE) stipulates that school districts must have a code of conduct policy. However, this policy may only impose certain types of discipline. For example, the following are consequences that schools in New York State may opt to use:

- Verbal warning
- Written warning
- Written notification to parents or guardians
- Probation
- Reprimand
- Detention
- Suspension from transportation
- Suspension from participation in athletic events
- Suspension from social or extracurricular activities
- Suspension from other privileges
- Exclusion from a particular class
- In-school suspension
- Involuntary transfer
- Suspension not in excess of five days
- Suspension in excess of five days

Departments of education from each state provide their districts with specific policy guiding disciplinary measures befitting the needs of their communities. However, even the best-laid plans are ineffective unless all those involved are knowledgeable of the program. Individual schools, as well as entire school districts, must make certain that the students, parents, and all faculty members are aware of the policy regarding discipline.

Moreover, all players must be willing to uniformly put into practice the plans of the program. If some faculty members do not follow the guidelines set forth by the district or school classroom management plan, students will not know how to interpret the mixed signals.

It is the administrator who continually exhibits the qualities of a successful school leader (Langley & Jacobs, 2006) that guides his staff to be good role models. Should some teachers fall lax as pertains to following certain regulations, such as demerits for an unexcused tardy arrival to class, students grow to expect other teachers to adopt the same attitude. This not only causes confusion for the students but also can be rather chaotic for a smooth-running, successful classroom management program.

Instructional techniques have been modified countless times as we continue to look for the best way to help children learn. According to Tharpe and Gallimore (1992), "The effective teacher movement [based on process and product research] has succeeded in identifying existing classroom practices associated with great student learning" (p. 15).

Effective classrooms are reliant on successful classroom management techniques. Duff and colleagues (as cited in Tharpe & Gallimore, 1992) state that teachers "spend most of their time monitoring to be sure the pupils are on task" (p. 16). Further study shows that "people would dispute the value of highly organized, technical and direct forms of didactic instruction." This type of teaching can only be realized with efficient classroom management and only with the support of leaders who are versed in good disciplinary techniques.

Finally, we must revisit the old cliché that idle hands are the tools of the devil. While a good lesson plan should still be viewed as a top priority for a teacher when forming her classroom management program, it is only a part of the process. Almost all of the ideas we have presented to this point incorporate actions taken by teachers but with involvement of administrators and parents. These people are instrumental in the formation and implementation of a good classroom management plan, which is why we have included them thus far and devoted individual chapters of this book to each. However, perhaps the single most important thing a teacher can do without assistance from others is to develop a lesson plan that is both interesting and engaging.

We often talk about the need to have a bag of tricks that includes enough variety to keep the lesson moving at a fast pace—to maintain the interest of all types of learners. Education experts such as Marzano (2001) and Tomlinson (1999) remind us that today's student population does indeed present the need for classroom activities to move along at a faster pace than in previous generations. Television programming is far more complex than shows of the early baby boomer years. When baby boomers began watching television, programs were designed as entertainment. However, the fast pace and complex plots of television shows today require much more cognitive reaction than in the past.

In the course of a sixty-minute program, more or less the time of a normal class, the viewer is presented with several problems (such as in an episode of *House*), a multitude of distractions from subplots and short-lived characters (as one encounters on *The Simpsons* or *Lost*), references to information gained from previous shows or seasons (as in *The West Wing* or soap operas), introductions to advanced terminology that plays an important role in the plot (as in *ER*), and interruption in the thought process from paid commercials.

Video and computer games have come a long way from the days of Pac Man and Pong. Players are engaged in complex story plots.

They must make split-second, life-and-death decisions for games such as those in the Star Wars series. Dexterity is essential for the complicated, fast-paced games. And although many adults may argue that the music of today's youth might lack in melodic complexity or diversity, the lyrics are most definitely quite involved and have a purposeful message.

If students are able to keep up with today's television shows, movie plots, video games, and music, they most certainly are not apt to sit through a long, tedious lesson or lecture. On the other hand, they are quite ready to handle multitasking in the classroom. They have been programmed to engage several parts of their metacognitive skills at once. Students thrive on trying to figure out what comes next. They have developed memory banks that store many small bits of information and know how to relate that information to the problem at hand.

It is now the task of the teacher to reach deep down into that bag of tricks to find new methods to keep children an active part of the learning process. Spectators do not excel in today's schools—participators, however, do. Have we not noticed that although game shows such as *Jeopardy!* and *Who Wants to Be a Millionaire?* are not terribly exciting, students go to great lengths to try to beat out their peers during games like these that have been tailored to fit the current curriculum?

Once we are certain that we have selected the best activities and put together an effective lesson plan, we must develop a means to ensure that we are in fact making progress. Regularly checking our progress is essential in order to ensure that we do not stray from our goals. One way to monitor progress is via a self-assessment tool. We offer one such tool at the end of this chapter.

With that in mind, this guide might be used as a tool to help teachers take a step back and answer the questions "What is happening?" and "What would I like to be happening?" in his or her classroom. Changes can be easily made by leaving out questions that do not fit in a particular school or conversely by adding questions that might be more pertinent to a specific site.

In addition to periodic checklists, it can be very useful for teachers to create a checklist for the beginning of each school year. While some questions are specific to each site, we offer as a suggestion a second checklist that can be used as is or to help develop a list that is personally tailored to fit your classroom as you set up for the new school year.

Checklists such as these enable the teacher to put together appropriate plans for success. Starting off the year well prepared and with participation in school activities and committees affords the teacher a good understanding of school district policies and building procedures. Working together with the entire faculty and developing as well as implementing a solid classroom management program greatly assist the new and veteran teacher.

Another component of our classroom management program is students who are classified as having special needs such as a 504 provision (Section 504 of the Rehabilitation Act of 1973); an individual education plan (IEP); or physical, mental, or emotional disabilities. These children need special attention in raising test scores and in general instruction. Additionally, we must adjust our classroom management plan not only to raise their academic achievement but also to maintain an atmosphere that is organized.

For example, some IEPs indicate what modifications are necessary to help keep the student on track or to be able to hear or see all that he needs in the room. If we have already set up our classrooms in a manner that provides an optimum learning environment, we should be able to accommodate these requirements with minimal effort. IEPs might also point out such things as what types of instruction are necessary or will aid a teacher in helping the student progress, thereby decreasing the child's inattentiveness in a new classroom.

A teacher who has a successful classroom management plan can accommodate any special needs without compromising the education and attention given to the other students in the class who do not have special needs. In order to accomplish this, general education teachers are encouraged to work closely with special education teachers, the special education aides assigned to the student, counselors, case workers, and administrators. Administrators must schedule workshops in the school-year calendar to assist the general education teacher in this area.

Working with the case managers of those who have been classified is one way to help understand the needs of the children and in many cases the parents of those students. We cannot overstress the importance of the general education teacher's maintaining this dialogue. There are many websites available to help the general education teacher learn to work successfully with children with special needs. We have listed several for you in the references and further resources section.

Once more, it is also important to mention here that we cannot assume that parents are aware of the material available to assist them with their child's education. It is our duty as educators to ensure that parents have access to such resources. At parent–teacher conferences or during communication such as via e-mail or telephone, a teacher should be able to direct a parent to professional written material, such as that provided on the various websites, to help them help us help their child.

Teachers, aides, and administrators must work together to ensure that we are taking advantage of the state and federal funds directed at preservice and in-service programs designed to instruct educators on working successfully with students who have disabilities; that aides are included in the lesson planning sessions; and that administrators develop a schedule that is conducive to a learning environment for special education and general education students, classroom teachers, and special education teacher aides.

Checklist for Teachers at the Beginning of the School Year

_____ My classroom is arranged in a manner free of extraneous distractions.

_____ My classroom is set to accommodate students who have special needs.

_____ Supplies are kept in a secure yet accessible area.

_____ I have placed orders for sufficient texts, supplies, and furnishings.

_____ I am familiar with the text and program of studies for this year.

_____ I have put together a personal set of materials to supplement the text.

_____ I am beginning the first day with two weeks of lesson plans written out.

_____ I know where the guide is for the grading system and am familiar with it.

_____ I have prepared a welcome letter for students and parents.

_____ I have updated our website to explain the course and expectations.

_____ I am familiar with our school plan and mission statement.

_____ I have read over our guidelines for students' rights and responsibilities.

_____ I have volunteered for at least one school committee.

_____ I have a desk/wall calendar where I can easily record important information or activities.

_____ I have a list of reliable substitutes readily available.

_____ I have set aside a spot with "anytime" substitute plans and instructions.

_____ My grading system is clearly explained to students and parents.

Checklist for Teachers to Help Monitor Progress

_____ I am pleased with the turnout I have for parent–teacher conferences.

_____ I respect students' comments, opinions, and ideas.

_____ I attend scheduled faculty meetings.

_____ I attend workshops, in-services, and seminars to remain current on classroom management issues.

_____ I provide parents current information on parenting issues relating to classroom management.

_____ I regularly check websites and written material regarding classroom management updates.

_____ I send home student work for parent review and comment.

_____ I solicit assistance from parents to provide supplies, expertise, and so on.

_____ I keep parents advised of positive comments and progress.

_____ I assign homework that requires family involvement.

_____ I provide parents with the tools they need to help with homework.

_____ I make myself visible to help monitor student activity in hallways and other areas of the school.

_____ I keep the school website current with class information.

_____ I post homework on the homework hotline daily.

_____ I return student assignments in a timely manner.

_____ I attend school-sponsored extracurricular activities.

2

THE ROLE OF ADMINISTRATORS

Teachers, as the frontline contact with students, certainly have an important role in assuring that students understand the discipline policy. The role of the administrator is to provide the time needed to disseminate this information.

Principals play an important role in both the organizational and political aspects of running a school as well as in promoting a positive learning environment for staff and students. The need for administrators to come into the classroom and hallways is an important action that must not be overlooked when formulating an effective and successful classroom management plan.

The presence of administrators sends the message that the school building is operating as a single unit rather than an atmosphere of "us and them." Breaking this negative barrier instills a feeling of trust and safety in students, thereby diverting their subconscious efforts toward positive actions such as their academic concerns and improved classroom and hallway behavior.

Classrooms are not the only areas where an administrator's presence is important. The presence of administrators in the hallways between class changes and frequent visits into classrooms, if done properly, can send a powerful and positive message to teachers. A few minutes should be set aside each day to roam the corridors, pop into restrooms, and walk around the outside of the building. If administrators are not normally assigned cafeteria duty, brief visits to the lunchroom can make a strong, positive statement.

A successful leader helps teachers identify and rectify situations that could result in an atmosphere where classroom management becomes an impossible chore. However, the administrator is not an exclusive leader. Effective administrators understand how to exercise their well-developed strong, positive interpersonal skills (Langley & Jacobs, 2006) in order to be the guide on the side.

It is essential that administrators delegate responsibility—such as giving a teacher room to be responsible for running his or her classroom—but without detaching themselves from the learning process. Teachers will be successful if they feel they are in charge of their classrooms but also realize that they are not alone. Support from administrators can arguably be the single strongest influence on a teacher's ability to maintain a successful classroom management program.

The same can be said for the relationship between a principal and the assistant principal (AP). Quite frequently, principals delegate all or most of the responsibility of student discipline to APs, stepping in only when a situation becomes serious enough to involve possible court action.

Additionally, principals often rely on APs to oversee certain departmental duties such as handling curricula items and scheduling. Therefore, it is important, based on the demands of the AP's job and his or her ability to prioritize responsibilities, that one understand that APs must themselves be successful managers. Furthermore, the AP must be a manager who can carry out the expectations of the principal while maintaining a good rapport with teachers, parents, and students. Keeping in mind that the duties of the AP include closely working with students and parents, it is in the best interest of the AP to keep abreast of the needs of the entire community.

When delegating responsibility for classroom management to an AP, the principal must first consider distribution of tasks so that the AP's time is spent providing the best possible support for the school community as a whole. An AP should be expected to assist in teacher evaluation but must not become detached from the principal in doing so. Also, an AP should certainly be a key player when it comes to classroom management, but it must never be forgotten that classroom management is a group effort that requires input, action, and support from all parts of the group—administrators, teachers, counselors, parents, and students.

To ensure that students, as well as teachers, understand expected student behavior and subsequent consequences, administrators must incorporate time into the master schedule to go over these topics. Some of the many successful methods employed around the country include the following:

- During opening week of each school year, students receive a copy of the code of conduct policy. Administrators, such as guidance counselors and assistant principals, conduct an assembly of groups of students in which the administrators present the information presented in the policy book. The presentation can be delivered like a lecture, but it is more effective if at least some role-playing activity is involved. After the presentation, teachers—such as homeroom teachers—review the information with their students, and a quizlike activity is performed. After the students have filled in their quiz answers, the class as a whole reviews each point and discusses the policy.

- A few minutes is set aside at the beginning of each grading quarter to review the code of conduct policy. The activity includes a quick looking over of the policy handbook, followed by discussion in which students express their understanding of each of the rules and regulations.

- Periodically throughout the school year, students perform little skits to emphasize specific points of the policy. The skits are presented as assembly productions or via the in-school television programming.
- The district presents a variety of programs to the general public via the district's television network. The information may be disseminated in the form of a written message that scrolls on the television screen, by oral presentation such as a lecture, or by informal or indirect messaging via locally or professionally performed skits.
- Student representatives in a high school in Florida meet frequently with the school administrators to discuss their code of conduct. Results of the meeting are delivered on the school morning television program. Administrators give permission for students to hang many flyers around the school either announcing any changes or as a reminder of expected behavior. High school students are often best reached by using a little humor. Keeping that in mind, messages such as the code of conduct flyers are taped to the vending machines, in the restrooms, all over the hallways, in the stairwells, and so on. This may not seem either humorous or new, but one thing it does accomplish is to catch the attention of the entire student body—and better still, spark conversation, thereby getting the students to partake in and show awareness of their responsibilities. So, what makes their method humorous or more effective than some? The flyers are hung upside down, placed on the floor, attached to student lockers—anywhere that is unique and eye-catching!

Another means by which an administrator can ensure that all faculty, students, and parents are well informed of the school or district policy on discipline and responsibilities is to provide students with a hard copy. For example, administrators can set aside funds to distribute student planner or agenda notebooks to students. While these notebooks are an excellent way for students to keep record of their assignments, a good notebook should include reference material such as maps or math tables as well as the responsibilities and expectations of students.

Ormond Stone Middle School in Fairfax, Virginia, took the use of the student planners a step further to assist in a variety of classroom management topics. Principal Kenneth A. Gaudreault, with the input of the entire faculty, devised a page for the school planner that serves as a hall pass. When students need to be out of the classroom, teachers need only enter their destination and the date and time the student left the room on an ongoing log sheet.

There are separate pages for each grading quarter. Students do not leave the classroom for unnecessary ventures because they understand that if the page is filled before the end of the quarter, short of an emergency, they are not permitted to leave the classroom during class time until the next quarter.

On the other side of each of these hall passes, there is a page for each quarter that is devoted to keeping track of student behavior. Rules of the school—such as being tardy, chewing gum, lacking homework assignments—are listed on this page, along with a chart on which points are deducted for infractions committed and a column to accumulate points to award outstanding performance. The page includes a list of consequences that accompany a specified number of points each grading quarter. For example, if a student loses twenty points, his or her parents receive a phone call to advise them of the student's behavior. A loss of thirty points will result in a detention (see figure 2.1).

In another district, the planner system was utilized in yet another manner. A message of a bomb threat was detected on one of the bathroom walls. Administrators checked the student planners to ascertain which students may have had the opportunity to visit that particular restroom during the school day.

Finally, one cannot overlook the value of a student agenda wherein the students record their homework assignments. One

S.T.A.R. Card

Students Taking Active Responsibility

Name: _____   Team: _____   1st Quarter

The S.T.A.R. Card is designed to reinforce positive work habits. Keeping your planner in good condition is also your responsibility. YOU MAY NOT REMOVE, COLOR, DRAW, OR CHANGE YOUR STAR CARD IN ANY WAY. Doing so will result in consequences and cost of a new planner.

Positive Points

Positive points can be added (2 points at a time, maximum of 4 per week) for actions that *exemplify* the Stone Student Commitments:

1) Accept responsibility for your education and decisions.
2) Put forth your best effort in meeting your responsibilities.
3) Act with honesty, respect, and compassion.
4) Support your fellow students and your teachers.
5) Ensure the safety of self, others, and property.
6) Arrive on time and prepared. Participate responsibly.

Point Record

100	99	98	97	96	95	94	93
92	91	90	89	88	87	86	85
84	83	82	81	80	79	78	77
76	75	74	73	72	71	70	69
68	67	66	65	64	63	62	61
60	59	58	57	56	55	54	53
52	51	50	49	48	47	46	45
44	43	42	41	40	39	38	37
36	35	34	33	32	31	30	29
28	27	26	25	24	23	22	21

Bonus Point Record

Week 1. _____
Week 2. _____
Week 3. _____
Week 4. _____
Week 5. _____
Week 6. _____
Week 7. _____
Week 8. _____
Week 9. _____

Subtotals: Week 1 ___ Week 2 ___ Week 3 ___ Week 4 ___ Week 5 ___ Week 6 ___ Week 7 ___ Week 8 ___ Week 9 ___ Week 10 ___

Negative Points

Points can be deducted for actions that make it more difficult for you or others to learn. Two points will be subtracted for each infraction unless otherwise noted:

1) Disruptive behavior.
2) Unprepared for class.
3) Incomplete or missing homework.
4) Cheating or copying work (6 points).
5) Tardiness
6) Chewing gum or carelessness with school equipment / supplies.
7) Disrespect or insubordination.
8) No Star Card (4 points).
9) Lost/Torn out Star Card (10 points)

The following steps will be taken if your point total falls to:
80 points   Phone Call   Date: _____
70 points   Detention   Date: _____
Parent Signature Required:
Detention Served: _____ (Teacher's Initials)
60 points   Loss of Star Card Celebration and written reflection
50 points   TLA Assignment, parent notified by administration
40 points   Friday Service 3–7 pm; intervention conference with parents

Tardy Record

| Team Advisory |
| Period 1 |
| Period 2 |
| Period 3 |
| Period 4 |
| Period 5 |
| Period 6 |
| Period 7 |
| Comments |

Figure 2.1 STAR Card to record student progress and to enforce compliance with school rules, regulations, and consequences. Source: Kenneth A. Gaudreault, Fairfax County Public Schools, Virginia

component of a good classroom management program is to ensure that students know their assigned work and that it is completed. Parents of students who are lax in doing their homework can request that teachers initial the agenda at the point where the student left off writing the assignment before leaving class. Once the student is at home, when the parent inquires whether the student has homework, a quick glance at the teacher's initials in the planner makes it virtually impossible for the child to claim that there is no homework or upcoming test/quiz/project for a particular class. Likewise, a teacher can request that the parent initial the student planner to let the teacher know that the parent is aware of the student's assignments. A student who keeps up with his homework and studying is well prepared for class and less likely to become a behavior issue.

The Schools Against Violence in Education Act (SAVE) in New York State has set guidelines on removing students from classrooms. Part of this act assures that teachers do not resolve poor classroom management programs simply by removal of a student that is disruptive. This is not to say that administrators are never to intervene by removing a particularly disruptive student. There is a definition of when students might have to be pulled from a class or removed from school, and we are responsible, as educators, to be familiar with such rules.

**Talk to Teachers before
Sending Disruptive Students Back to Class**

Have you ever sent an unruly student to the principal's office only to see him return, smug and triumphant, in just a couple of minutes? Those of you who say no, appreciate how fortunate you are. Those of you who say yes—a thousand times yes—will be pleased to know of a solution proposed by a Maryland state legislator. Delegate Terry Gilleland, a 29-year-old former student member of his local school board, thinks that principals should be required, by law, to meet face-to-face with the

(continued)

teacher before sending the student back to the classroom. Maryland already has a law requiring the principal to confer with the teacher—but
as teachers everywhere know, principals too often just send a note
back with the student. A reasonable criticism of this law could be: Can't
this be handled without another law? And we'd like to think the answer
is yes. Unfortunately, the Maryland principals' association argued that
scheduling a meeting with the teacher simply wasn't feasible, given the
teacher's and principal's schedules! Of course, in the long run, the principal isn't saving any time by shirking the duty to discipline students and
confer with teachers: When a trip to the principal's office means nothing more than a five-minute break from class, students' behavior dete-
riorates drastically. The bill didn't pass. The fact that it was even proposed is a reminder: Student discipline can't be solved if teachers don't
get backed up. ("Talk to Teachers," 2006)

Taking a look at the case of Terry Gilleland, we note that some
states clearly indicate what actions can be taken and the role of the
administrator. For example, according to SAVE, a student must be
given an opportunity to present her version of the relevant events
that caused her to be removed from a class. The teacher must complete a referral form and meet with the appropriate administrator
before the end of that day, if possible, or within twenty-four hours
of the removal. Within forty-eight hours, the administrator must
notify a parent in writing, giving the reason for the removal and ac-
knowledging the right of the parent to an informal meeting.

When repeated offenses make it necessary to remove a student
from a particular class, or classes, the district should provide an alternative course of studies for the benefit of the student. These
programs, based on the severity of the offense, can range from after-
school programs to alternative schools. The support of the administrator in these circumstances is important but must be used spar-
ingly.

Another course of action currently utilized in many schools is
one in which administrators make many unscheduled mini-visits to

all classrooms throughout the entire school year. These mini-visits (or mini-observations) are not meant to have the principal or other administrators micromanage the teachers. The role of the principal in a very effective school is that of an instructional leader—doors cannot be closed, keeping the classroom activities away from the rest of the school climate. Likewise, doors should not be used to keep the rest of the school in the dark as to what is happening inside the classroom.

Mini-observations should take place often in order to allow the observer to form an accurate picture of the class in session and how the students act or react on different days. There is no magic number of how frequently the visits should occur. However, they should be conducted often, with the absolute number dictated by the individual school based on issues such as teacher contracts and the number of problems that need attention. The number of visits should never be based on the amount of time an administrator can devote to this activity. A successful school puts the overall welfare of the students as a top priority.

The practice of mini-observations does not mean that the shift of control moves to the principal. The teacher still maintains the position of leader in the classroom. The role of the principal is that of a participant, not a manager. One must keep in mind that teachers need to actually see that their principal has an interest in their work. The occasional "thumbs up" does not require much effort, does not cost anything, and is very important for a teacher to receive from his principal from time to time.

The purpose of these frequent mini-observations goes beyond mere development of a closer working relationship between teacher and administrator. The visits give administrators the opportunity to assess all aspects of the goings-on in the classroom—instruction, discipline, logistics, and so on. Additionally, the presence of an administrator, even for a brief minute or two, may refocus student attention on the lesson, thereby facilitating the teacher's role in classroom management.

The presence of administrators, even for these brief visits, sends a message to students wherein they recognize the fact that the administration is aware of and cares about the students' progress, well-being, and overall achievement. As with adults, children have a strong need for constant feedback of their progress. Teachers provide this feedback in the form of results of tests, quizzes, homework, projects, and class participation. Principals can provide a means of feedback by their presence in the classroom.

A mini-observation does not mean that an administrator enters the room unnoticed, watches from the door for a few minutes, and then disappears. With as little disruption as possible, the administrator should walk around the room and peer over the shoulders of the students to see what they are working on. If the students are working on a project or writing exercise, a few words of praise go a long way.

Depending on the activity during a mini-observation, the principal can make note of specific instances of academic or behavioral excellence on the part of one or more of the students. Soon after the class visit, preferably before the end of the day, while passing in the hall or the cafeteria or out on the school grounds, the principal should make it a point to make a comment to the student about her exemplary behavior.

For example, as a student is waiting to board the school bus, a statement such as "Mary, I was really impressed by how you answered that very difficult question in math today—good job" does not take much effort but builds confidence and an overall good feeling for the student. It is important for the students to know that they have a main office that cares.

The result of a brief mini-observation should bring some words of encouragement and constructive criticism to the teacher. Administrators should demonstrate overt concern by supporting the teachers. Students need to see that the teachers and administrators are a single unit, while at the same time actions should never be taken to send the message of you versus us. Students have a right and a need to be shown that they are part of the entire learning community.

The proactive administrator gains the confidence and respect of students and teachers, creating an environment that is conducive to learning, with very few incidents of undesirable behavior. Frequent visibility of the administrators can and should serve as a positive sign. Students and teachers should be advised that, over the course of the school year, they should expect to see an administrator enter their classrooms for several unannounced mini-observations.

Administrators should stress the fact that these observations are a positive action wherein they are afforded a firsthand look at what matters most—the students and their learning process. Mini-observations, or pass-through visits, should be designed to provide students and teachers with the reassurance that their administrators care about what goes on in the classroom. These visits should never be a vehicle to admonish a teacher, single out a student for misbehaving or chastise the entire group, or any other punitive action. Matters of a negative manner should always be conducted in a neutral setting and as privately as possible.

Generally speaking, it is not good practice to convey negative comments unless it can be done face to face. Even the best-intended criticism can come across as a harsh reprimand if left to an impersonal note or e-mail message. Use of a camcorder to record a short message can be one means to send a video e-mail. Similarly, one might opt to create an old-fashioned video and drop it in the mailbox of the teacher. Finally, a short e-mail can suffice, but only if it delivers good news.

Using either of these methods might be helpful in situations where schedules do not provide sufficient common time for a personal meeting. While sending a teacher a video message conveys sentiment more accurately than the written word, the preferred method of passing along any news is with a face-to-face meeting, even if it is for five minutes.

Additionally, it is important to note that comments by an administrator to the teacher must be made as soon as possible after a mini-visit. A personal meeting is not necessary.

No matter which method is used, immediate feedback is essential. Failure to do so might raise doubt as teachers begin to wonder if the news is so bad that the administrator is waiting for a period of free time that is long enough to deliver the news and initiate subsequent conversation.

Additionally, unscheduled mini-observations allow administrators to see teachers and students interacting in a natural setting. When teachers know that an administrator is coming for a scheduled observation, no matter how hard they try to act naturally, it is human nature to make sure that we look our best. Therefore, teachers might be inclined to put forth lesson plans that are not necessarily the normal order of business. More often than not, this results in a fake reality setting. Students and keen administrators are quick to catch on about how the teacher tried to set the tone. Observations are designed not to see a staged performance but to see the real world and offer praise and advice as warranted.

Traditional scheduled observations often last for half or whole periods. In this amount of time, students can change their behavior to act as they think they should, or worse for the teacher, students have time to misbehave. On the other hand, brief mini-observations do not give students the time to react to the visit. They, as well as the teacher, are more apt to behave as they normally would.

By making many brief visits to all classes, administrators see how each child behaves in different settings, with different teachers. This can provide valuable information for team meetings as well as parent conferences. Such a revelation should lead to the formulation of a plan for the individual student in which future unaccepted behavior is prevented from having a chance to develop.

An instructional strategy for one teacher may not attain the same results with the same students as it might for another. Providing time for the teachers to conduct many visits to observe other class-rooms, especially to try to form an accurate picture of one particu-larly challenging student, can be an unattainable goal. The admin-istrator, by making a series of mini-observations of all the classes of the student in question, can put pieces of the whole picture in place and discuss the situation with each teacher.

Professional learning communities and grade-level team meet-ings provide a venue for this type of interchange of information and strategies. However, the unbiased observations from one who has the opportunity to see, not react with, a student from class to class provides the best report. This unbiased person is the admin-istrator who does not have ownership of the lesson plan; nor does she have such close, daily interaction with the student in question.

Gaining the input of the entire staff when putting together or re-vising schoolwide rules not only makes the task easier but also cre-ates a willingness among teachers to comply. However, the fastest way to ensure that teachers will be reluctant or negligent in carry-ing through rules—such as punitive action for student misbehav-ior—is to give the impression that the administrators are not sup-porting the teachers.

If a student's behavior becomes so disruptive that the teacher's only recourse is to have the student removed from the classroom, the administrator only demeans and alienates the teacher if the ad-ministrator does not take the incident as seriously as the teacher does. The only way to truly understand the frustration experienced by the teacher is to speak with him as soon as possible. This action should not be taken during the class period in question so as not to prolong the attention or distraction by the other students. How-ever, the meeting should take place within a very short time after the incident.

Should a teacher reprimand a disruptive or insubordinate stu-dent and send that student to the office, the administrator should support the teacher's action. It is important that the student believe the teachers and administrators are on the same page. Naturally, at times teachers and administrators might have differing opinions on the severity of a student issue. To avoid creating a scene where the student might interpret this difference of opinion as a weakness in the system, the administrator and teacher involved must come to a consensus. This should be done before the administrator delivers his decision for action to the student, but not in the presence of the student.

If the student's unacceptable behavior is beyond routine, the administrator should meet with the student and teacher before making a decision on how to handle the matter. By doing so, all three are afforded the opportunity to review the accusation, examine the possible events leading to such behavior, and reach an agreement on the punitive action to be taken.

Just as one parent should never downplay the importance of her partner when making decisions about a child's life, particularly in front of the child, administrators should not come between the relationship of the teacher and the student.

Punitive action should be fair and uniform. If, for example, a school rule states that any student caught vandalizing school property will be issued a three-day in-school suspension, the punishment must be applied in all cases. If student A marks the hall walls with washable crayons while student B does the same but with indelible ink, more leniency should not be afforded to student A by the appropriate administrator.

By the same token, the punishment, while it should not be downplayed, should also fit the crime. Whenever possible, the punishment should have a tie to the infraction. For example, a student who vandalizes the school walls might be instructed to help the custodial staff clean the school building directly after school for two or three hours on Friday afternoons. Or, if your custodial staff works on Saturdays, one Saturday spent cleaning a school rather than enjoying the company of friends or participating in a sporting event could serve as a great deterrent for repeat offenders.

A student that constantly disrupts a class might understand the errors of her ways if that student's punishment is to help run the class. One way to accomplish this is to assign homework to the student wherein he is required to compose ten questions to review the day's lesson. The next day, that student would have to lead the class in the warm-up exercise. This could be carried out for as few as one day or for as long as it seems necessary to allow the student to appreciate the need for students to respond to teachers.

A student caught stealing or cheating might be given a job to do after school, such as helping the office staff by emptying trash cans, sharpening pencils, filing, or cleaning out the lost-and-found box. Perhaps the duties might extend to the school grounds to clean the area, rid any garden areas of weeds, assist the P.E. teachers setting up outdoor equipment, and so on.

Keeping in touch with the students is only a portion of a good classroom management plan for principals. An effective principal also is aware of the concerns of his staff. One way to accomplish this is by setting brief monthly faculty meetings. Meetings should be scheduled for the same time each month (e.g., the second Thursday). They should begin directly after school lets out and have a time limit of no more than perhaps one hour.

By making these meetings part of the normal routine, they are more apt to achieve high attendance rates by the entire staff. A good, solid agenda that is shared with the faculty before the meeting also helps maintain attendance and gives the entire staff time to prepare for the month's topic.

At monthly faculty meetings, a time should be set for recognition of accomplishments. Perhaps a token gift could be presented such as a certificate or an inexpensive yet meaningful item—a coffee mug, something for the classroom, a book. In addition to this portion of the meeting, time should be set aside wherein a previously selected—perhaps via a schedule set at the beginning of the school year—department can share something with the rest of the faculty.

For this segment, perhaps members of each department can explain their curriculum and seek suggestions for additional cross-curricula activities. Additionally, a department might wish to present new findings in educational techniques that members of that department might have acquired via their district-level workshops.

There are many actions school leaders can take to encourage and support personnel. For example, successful principals have created teams with areas of expertise to which others can turn, developed systems and structures to collect and disseminate knowledge, benchmarked against other successful organizations, and developed a culture of overall enrichment. Some specific actions include the following:

- Creating leadership teams and action teams
- Tracking key performance indicators over time
- Implementing an open-door policy for all
- Soliciting parent and community input
- Implementing joint parent–student teacher conferences
- Increasing release time for planning and collegial discussions
- Initiating focus groups and book studies of relevant issues

---

Checklist for Administrators

_____ I follow our policy and regulations regarding student discipline without bias and on a timely basis.

_____ I ensure that students and teachers are aware of our rules and regulations and their subsequent consequences.

_____ I include student, teacher, and parent input when putting together our rules and regulations and their subsequent consequences.

_____ I frequently conduct mini-observations.

_____ After mini-observations, I give useful feedback to the teachers.

_____ After mini-observations, I make it a point to recognize student achievement.

_____ I interact with the entire student body by making myself visible.

_____ I am aware of the overall atmosphere of the school and try to prevent classroom management from becoming too difficult for the teachers.

_____ The entire staff was instrumental in setting the school plan.

_____ The entire staff works together in a professional learning community.

_____ I model the expectations that I have of my staff.

_____ The building site is arranged to provide a safe learning environment.

_____ My administrative staff supports the actions of my faculty.

_____ I keep parents informed of school rules and regulations.

_____ I attend parent–teacher conferences.

_____ I support my faculty when they carry out the school plan.

_____ I hold monthly faculty meetings to allow the exchange of ideas and concerns as well as to inform the staff of new information.

_____ I invite each department or component of my school to actively participate in monthly faculty meetings.

_____ I have ensured that each department is represented on our task force.

THE ROLE OF PARENTS

A survey sponsored by the Parent Teacher Student Association (PTSA) and *Newsweek* (May, 1993) reported that parents and school personnel did not feel they were working well together on behalf of the children. How, one asks, can administrators fix that? How can we help teachers if in fact there is a lack of trust between schools, teachers, parents, and districts? Perhaps part of the answer begins with site-based committees or teams, coffee with the principal, and other events that bring the community to the school and the school to the community.

In a very creative book titled *You Can't Scare Me . . . I Have a Teenager*, the authors Thomas W. Stacy and David A. Gold (2005) state that the relationship between parent and school is one that needs continual work. Parents who pressure teachers to instruct in a certain way or to do particular learning activities with the class only disenfranchise the interaction between student, teacher, and parents, further causing stress and nonproductivity.

When there is a concern or problem, showing the teacher or principal that you are not trying to blame anyone but are willing to work with the school helps to alleviate the situation. It is here where an administrator could aid in the process of rebuilding the bridge between teacher and parent.

Nonetheless, there are certain issues that although taught in school are generally more successful if the parental role is the strongest factor. One such issue is that of building good moral and ethical character from a very young age. In addition to instructing children to become good citizens, parents must also play a major role in modeling these beliefs to their children. These kinds of behaviors should be first taught at home and then reinforced in the school setting by role-modeling teachers, administrators, and peers.

First Lady Laura Bush, in support of her husband's stand on education, is a strong advocate for improving character education in our schools. In an October 2002 joint effort between the U.S. Department of Education and Court TV concerning character and community, Mrs. Bush announced the distribution of $16.7 million in grants to assist communities to provide students with lessons that promote high moral character.

President George W. Bush made it clear in his 2002 and 2003 State of the Union Addresses that character education is to be an integral part of our education system. As part of this initiative, he created the USA Freedom Corps to encourage Americans to volunteer two years or 4,000 hours during the course of their lives to become engaged in community services such as mentor programs.

Already in place were other programs such as AmeriCorps. Established in 1994, AmeriCorps provides volunteer services to mentor and promote positive and moral character in our youth. Another, Learn and Serve America, provides grants to support efforts to engage students in community service linked to academic achievement and the development of civic skills. This approach to education, called service learning, improves communities while preparing young people for a lifetime of responsible citizenship.

One might argue that character education starts in the classroom; others believe that this is the responsibility of the parents.

With one side waiting for the other to take action, there is a good possibility that both sides accomplish little or nothing. It is the responsibility of the school to make certain that parents understand that they must do their best to include positive moral character as part of the curriculum.

Years ago there was a quiet understanding that schools would teach those values shared by the community. Parents and teachers had a common vision of what those values and beliefs entailed. You may recall the many stories about parents who would support the teacher's punitive consequences for misbehavior and how the parents, to ensure that those "interruptions" by their child in class did not happen again, inflicted further punishment on the child. According to the teachers, those days, for better or worse, are gone. The nation's economic situation makes moving from one community to another necessary, thus taking those shared values of one community and replacing them with those of another.

Equally important is letting the parents know that they hold the most valuable duty as role model and character builder. Unfortunately, character education is all too often an area that parents are ill equipped to handle, are uncomfortable handling, or simply believe they do not have the time to handle. The responsibility now shifts toward the schools.

Citizens who are made to feel a part of the action are more often those who tend to become committed to the practices of positive moral character. They understand how to use their strong, positive interpersonal skills to successfully obtain desired goals (Langley & Jacobs, 2005). These citizens are also the most likely to exhibit their moral character in a manner that would foster similar behavior in their students.

While the primary agenda for education is raising a student's level of academic success, the hidden agenda of instilling moral character proves invaluable for creating positive classroom management. Such virtues as patience, responsibility, respect, honesty, and fortitude facilitate our programs of successful classroom management.

It is the responsibility of the school to ensure that parents who need or want direction to help their children are given the tools to do so. Parents must first be aware of the values being promoted by the school and then be given the guidance necessary to help them reinforce these ideas at home. In order to get to this point, educators must build a strong, positive working relationship between the school, the students, their families, and the community as a whole.

Studies show that students with a strong, positive character are also those who are more successful academically. In a book titled *Unfulfilled Expectations: Home and School Influences on Literacy* (Snow, Barnes, Chandler, Goodman, & Hemphill, 1991), the authors cite several research projects that demonstrate that family involvement in schools is most beneficial to student success.

Studies on academic achievement before and after the 1960s differ. The Coleman report (1966), a study initiated by Congress (1964 Civil Rights Act), is largely responsible for this newfound way of thinking. Basically, the Coleman Report states that the principal factor that affects student academic achievement is the specific characteristics in that student's family background. James Coleman's work was seen as an inaccurate study based on statistics. Nevertheless, his findings remain the basis for continued studies to date. Therefore, we can still operate under the premise that the impact of family background on student achievement might be the most accurate litmus test.

The report concludes that while the importance of the role of families in academic success is widely accepted in professional trade literature, it is not recognized as the most important in educational procedures.

There is no set formula or definition for the type and level of family involvement in our schools. Certain limits occur based on the general demographics of the school or district. Others are based on local, state, or national initiatives. No Child Left Behind (NCLB) and similar programs are directed toward overall academic improvement, while others concentrate on issues such as school safety. Changes in policy or laws set guidelines and define specific procedures that aid or restrict family involvement. Local laws may allow parents or guardians to serve on shared decision-making committees. All parents should play a major role in their legal obligation to ensure that students meet attendance requirements. Likewise, there are laws that set the standards for home schooling. Child welfare services work to ensure that children are brought up in positive, safe environments.

Conversely, there are no laws insisting that parents assist their children to be successful academically, in spite of the fact that studies show academic growth and family involvement go hand in hand. The reality is that when parents and schools work together, the outcome is favorable behavior and significantly higher tests scores.

The level and type of parental involvement vary depending on the level of academic success or the financial situation of the school or district. Often there is need for guidance and direction—building good character and social skills that must begin and continue at home. Sometimes, as in the case of many small districts and private or parochial schools where budgets may be limited, parent partnership is useful to help raise funds for certain activities. The goal is to identify the most important areas that would benefit from involving parents.

The key element of this type of communication and partnership extends the relationship of parents and ties the family to the school. If we subscribe to the belief that a student who takes ownership of his school will increase his success, we must extend that belief to the parents. Parents who feel that the school is an extension of their family are more apt to take part in the goings-on of the school and become involved in the education of their child.

Perhaps our first reaction is that it is a far stretch to think that schools are an extension of a family. However, when one looks at how many hours each day a student is at school compared with the waking hours they spend with parents, it is not that difficult to imagine. Taking this reality into consideration, it becomes more apparent that a little bonding between parents and schools should pay off in the end.

One might begin this bonding process via such avenues as the local PTA or PTSA. These groups have much success in many school districts around the country. Foremost, we must not forget that as is the case with almost anything, we get out of a PTSA what we put into it. To communicate successfully, to achieve what one sets out to accomplish, there must be good representation on the part of all parties. Clearly defined goals should be set and agreed upon, with the understanding and willingness to make changes as our student needs evolve.

PTSA groups are there for us to communicate—parents, teachers, and students—and should include anyone whose lives our students touch. These programs provide a venue to address a wide variety of topics. PTSA meetings should be an exchange of ideas. Perhaps the most crucial element at these meetings is the time devoted to reviewing policy on discipline and expected student behavior.

There are many ways teachers can work with parents to ensure that they take an active role in the lives of students both at home and in the school. Other than via PTSA meetings, there are school websites, e-mails and backpack letters to parents, gatherings such as Back to School Night, and parent–teacher conferences. Reminders of upcoming events, important dates, or short notices should be strategically placed outside of school buildings, such as on message boards, so that they are easily visible to parents as they drop off or pick up students or perhaps as they are driving past the school property. Additionally, representatives from the PTSA should be invited to partake in a school's professional learning community (PLC).

It might not be realistic to expect a PTSA representative to be available for every PLC meeting, particularly if those meetings are frequent and during the school day. However, the PTSA can be kept apprised of developments by keeping the lines of communication open. Their input for large decisions should be welcomed and taken seriously. Perhaps meetings that result in major changes in curriculum or other school matters should include a PTSA representative. Each school or district must evaluate its own situation and create a schedule that meets its needs and at the same time includes input from the PTSA.

As we enlist the assistance of parents in our classroom management plan, we must make certain that they are familiar with the many components of the school. Parents should be aware of cultural, linguistic, and gender differences. Again, these topics might vary to meet the demographics specific to an individual school or district. What transpires in the adult world may be very different from in a child's world.

Merely living and working in a culturally diverse atmosphere does not necessarily prepare parents to understand how their children interact in school. Efforts put forth by the teachers and administrators bring the parents closer to the goings-on in a school and thereby assist in the success of both the school climate and the community as a whole.

Instructing parents how to communicate with schools is vital for successful interaction, whether we are dealing with children or adults. Using previously learned knowledge, perhaps from their place of employment, parents may be accustomed to bringing personal concerns directly to management. Therefore, they may take the slightest issue of academic or behavioral concerns directly to a school-based or central office–based administrator rather than communicating first with the child's teacher. If it is your policy that parents first contact teachers regarding certain topics, those ideas must be clearly stated to parents.

A telephone or television cable wire that transmits information does not obtain optimum results if there is a kink in the wire. If you attempt to bypass certain steps—much like hot-wiring a car—you might make a connection, but there will be a loss in power or quality of service. The same analogies apply to communication between schools and families. If parents have concerns about grading or discipline issues between their child and a specific teacher, going straight to the principal will get a reaction, possibly even the results the parent thought they wanted. However, the lines of communication may have suffered from kinks in the wire, resulting in a loss of the quality of service.

Administrators must make it clear to parents that the teacher is the person with the most direct knowledge of the student in the school building and therefore the most logical person to go to with questions or complaints. Teachers have the responsibility to assure parents, and students, that they are ready to receive any contact from parents or students in the most professional way. Both parents and students must feel comfortable communicating with teachers. They must see that their concerns will be addressed without bias, negative attitude, or negative consequence to the student.

Communication is an essential component of survival. We can communicate in a variety of ways, such as through physical motions or symbols or through the use of language—expressed orally or through the written word. The use of language is, by far, the most commonly used form of communication. When we hear or read a word, we are free to form our own visual interpretation. Hopefully our interpretation is the same as the intention of the person who generated the message.

While teachers have, and should have, constant contact with parents, the leadership of administrators plays a larger role in enlisting the help of parents. How can educators aid the parents? The answer is not unlike the riddle of the chicken and the egg. Do we concentrate on educating parents regarding behavior of students, or do we place the emphasis on the school to educate the child? There are several theories that address which way we should direct our attention. To simplify our efforts, let us take a look at some of the issues that bring administrators to work together with parents.

Problems often arise when there is an absence of a traditional, Norman Rockwellian family unit or when parents or guardians are not in concert with schools in their prioritization of education. To get an idea of just how students react with adults in a role of authority, we contacted middle and high school students to get their input. Our research has shown that all to often children find these adult models less than desirable (alcoholics, workaholics, and so on), too authoritative, or afraid to be forthcoming on topics that children want to discuss such as drugs, sex, and other moral or social issues.

The students with whom we spoke stated that they look forward to contact with adults who do not have the personal relationship that causes them to judge and react unfavorably to the children—adults who are not so close to them or who may be biased, as in the case of their parents. They believe that it is easier to speak with some teachers than with parents, and they welcome the candor and friendship-like relationships that are often formed with adults at school. Many students look forward to attending school to bond with these adults.

While we do not wish to alienate students from their parents, we must remember the role of in loco parentis that we hold and be present for our students when they seek adult assistance. Guidance counselors, teachers, social workers, and other trained officials have the duty to ensure a child's well-being, should there be a need for intervention.

To further illustrate this point, we can look to the story of two gangs in an inner-city setting described in Jay MacLeod's (1995) book Ain't No Makin' It. The two gangs were a predominately white group of boys identified as the Hallway Hangers and a predominately African American group operating under the name of the Brothers.

The Brothers had a mixed relationship with their parents, some coming from broken homes, some from parents whose jobs kept them away from home, and others whose parents were present but were not model citizens. However, the parents took an active role in their sons' lives and taught their children values and the need for a good education. The result was that these boys were regular attendees at their school.

One has to wonder if they attended school not just for the academic gratification but also to form additional bonds with the adults there. Perhaps they saw their teachers as a nonjudgmental extension of their parents.

The Brothers accepted societal values, and their parents had a significant impact on their aspirations, both in the educational and occupational arenas. The Brothers were optimistic and viewed the opportunity structure as open, one that rewards ability and hard work. Similarly, this group demonstrated a tendency to conform to schooling, and their teachers became for them sources of direction whom they trusted and wanted to model.

The Hallway Hangers did not have the strong parental guidance that the Brothers enjoyed, and this lack of direction resulted in a negative attitude toward school, poor attendance, a high dropout rate, and overall discipline problems. The parents of the Hallway Hangers argued that their children were streetwise adults long before their time, and therefore they believed that trying to convince these kids to attend—and finish—school was a lost battle before even starting.

Johns Hopkins University professor Melvin Kohn's (1969) research concludes that families who demonstrate their own occupational success to their children transfer these same values and behaviors. By example, a working-class adult often follows the rules and regulations of a company or organization and is reluctant to challenge authority. Children of professional parents, however, are taught to challenge authority, negotiate, and consider options. Both sets of parental guidance prepare children for success as pertains to their family experiences.

Kohn also raises the interesting notion that sometimes parents have aptitude in certain areas, but other skills a child needs must be provided by trained educators. Kohn refers to this as knowledge constrain. In other words, parents may know what is good for their children but may not have the skills and knowledge to pass it on.

Generally speaking, parents want the best education for their child. They have a deep interest in the child's success both in academics and overall life experiences. Therefore, once parents are brought to realize that the best course of action is an atmosphere of cooperation between student, family, and school, the child is given the best possible opportunity to achieve success. But before proceeding, all parties must agree on the definition of success. All too often we tend to strive for success as it is perceived in our own hearts and minds. Consideration must be given to the needs and goals of all parties. A common goal must be identified before moving on.

Values and morals differ greatly. So do the time and place to work with parents, particularly when addressing classroom management issues. Working out those differences at a one-time event such as an "open house" (which really does not allow for a personal conference) makes it difficult to really resolve any classroom management issues. Therefore, topics such as these are best left to individual conferences. Individual conferences can involve a teacher, a student, and a parent or a student, a parent, a grade-level team, and an administrator or administrators, depending on the nature of the item to be discussed.

One thing to remember is that all issues are contributing factors to a successful classroom management program and therefore should not be shoved aside and forgotten. The lines of communication have to be open all of the time. Limited communication between school and parent can lead to serious differences in the way children are taught as well as disciplined. In addition, parental concepts that were in line with community standards for discipline and were deemed personally suitable by school legal officials may not be so in a new state (e.g., corporal punishment).

When parents or guardians may not be in concert with local school rules or concerns, this lack of coordination and cooperation becomes an issue that must be corrected via close connection with parents through a sound classroom management plan. We must examine how to successfully reach parents and assist them to see the importance of their involvement and to become part of the school's classroom management program. This is essential not only for academic success but also for behavioral issues. Therefore, the question becomes, how do we induce families to become involved in their children's education?

Administrators can and must initiate the lead to make parents aware of the value of the education of their children. A beginning would be to address specifically targeted parental groups and invite them to participate in school activities—particularly career day programs, parent–teacher–student conferences, extracurricular activities, volunteer programs, and so on.

We cannot stress enough the importance of maintaining a constant line of communication between parents and schools. All too often we see reports indicating that many parents are of the notion that teachers do not inform them of misbehavior or lower grades on report cards until it is too late. Although at times we may find that these parents are correct, we are obligated to do our best to ensure that these lines of communication are not weakened and that parents are not the last to find out information regarding their children's progress.

One action that some schools have employed successfully to involve more parents and guardians is signing a contract between the school and each family. While under no obligation on the part of the family, drawing up a contract just might be the motivating force in establishing a connection between family and school. At present there is no accountability to such a contract for conventional public schools, but one does exist for the charter schools within them.

Parent Contract

The parent(s)/guardian(s) of _____ have read and agree to abide by the following:

WHEREAS, the undersigned parent(s)/guardian(s) has made a personal decision to enroll my child(ren) at the Charter School of Excellence in order to provide my child with a unique educational opportunity;

WHEREAS, my desire and decision to enroll my child at the Charter School of Excellence is based upon my desire to become an active partner in the education of my child; and

WHEREAS, I recognize that the Charter School of Excellence is a public charter school of *choice* not entitlement;

NOW THEREFORE, in consideration of the foregoing;

1. As a parent of a student at the Charter School of Excellence, my commitment is to abide by the following rules and regulations adopted by the Board of Directors:

    To recognize and embrace my role as having primary responsibility for the education of my child.

    To attend all conferences scheduled with any member of the Charter School of Excellence staff.

    To participate in the Parent Volunteer Program, including volunteering twenty hours for one child and thirty hours for two or more children, at a capacity that is sensitive to the needs of the school.

    To provide transportation to and from school for my child. If I am late picking up my child, I understand that I will be charged for after-school care at whatever rate is in existence at that time. If my child is continually tardy, I understand that for the benefit of my child's education, he or she may be required to attend a school that is more accessible for my child.

    To purchase uniforms for my child from the Charter School of Excellence Board-approved supplier and ensure my child abides by the dress code of the Charter School of Excellence.

    To supply a healthy lunch and snack, either brown bagged or purchased from the Charter School of Excellence Board-approved vendor, each school day for my child.

(continued)

To be responsible for timely payment of any fees accrued to my account at the Charter School of Excellence.

To participate in the Charter School of Excellence Parent Teacher Resource Group meetings, which are scheduled monthly throughout the school year.

To encourage my child to abide by the Broward County Public School Code of Conduct, supplemented by the Cheetah Code of Conduct, by words and deeds of my own life.

2. In order to enhance my child's academic growth, I agree to do the following:

   A. To read and use information sent home by the school to keep parents informed of the academic topics to be introduced and studied in the classroom.
   B. To provide a suitable time and place within the home for homework.
   C. To assist my child in obtaining and regularly using a library card at the Public Library and to allow for thirty minutes of reading daily.
   D. To limit television and video games during the week and allow more time for reading, studying, and family time.
   E. To check my child's homework folder nightly.
   F To encourage my child to research his or her academic level with deep commitment and enthusiasm for learning.

I (We) understand that by not fulfilling my contractual obligations to the school and to my child, this will result in my child being suspended or withdrawn and referred to a regular public school or a private school of the parent's choice as approved by the Charter School of Excellence Board of Directors.

Signature of Parent/Guardian _____ Date _____

Signature of Parent/Guardian _____ Date _____

Acknowledged by _____ Date _____

—Robert Haag, President

The Charter School of Excellence (2003) has developed this contract to bring about a parental commitment to involvement in the educational process of each child. This, or similar contracts, can serve as a model that schools can modify to fit their particular circumstances.

If schools or districts use contracts such as this, perhaps the results would include a clearer picture of what changes must be implemented to involve parents and help students become successful. Family contracts can help inform parents of their responsibilities. They can promote the creation of positive relationships between schools and parents or guardians. They might focus on a variety of very specific issues such as attendance, parent volunteers, student requirements, behavioral issues, academics, problems and concerns, or any other topics that fit the needs of your school–parent relationship.

The family has the ultimate responsibility to monitor the progress of the child since no education law mandates that a parent or guardian become active in a child's education. It may be the wish of every educator that state education departments require parental involvement, but until that time, it is the parents who must, in the end, take an active interest.

The Charter School of Excellence is only one example of what a school–parent contract might look like. We found no set manner or documented literature that addresses the specifics of a school or parent and student contract. However, using such a device may serve many functions in addition to those we have already discussed. For example, contracting with the school to volunteer for a school committee, such as shared decision making, may help the parent form stronger relationships with teachers, staff members, and other families and parents. This type of interaction could help create a social atmosphere of "give and take," which might resolve many miscommunications between parents and teachers.

Of course the school district is also held responsible for keeping up its end of the bargain by informing parents about the progress of their children in not only behavioral situations but in the academics as well. Naturally, districts are required to inform parents about tardiness and absences when they occur, as well as all upcoming exams and whether children are adhering to the school's code of conduct. Schools should meet with parents not only during the specific open-house dates for parent conferences but also at any time that the parent requests or that the school district deems necessary.

Ensuring a positive relationship between teacher and parent and upholding an obligation between the two to follow through with the terms of the contract is to an extent the job of the school-based or central office administrator. If a teacher is upholding the contract and the parent is not, perhaps the best course of action might be to bring in the unbiased administrator to approach the parent. Naturally, if the parent is upholding her end but the teacher is not, the administrator is obligated to approach the teacher.

In either situation, the administrator must be prepared to enter a discussion, with the aim to come out with a win–win solution. The administrator must demonstrate support for the teacher while not alienating the parent. In the long run, strict adherence to the contract helps everyone involved develop a better relationship, resulting in a better student, a more effective teacher, and a prouder parent.

Use of tools such as contracts can be very specific and rather involved. This is not to say that less specific, less involved, and less directly targeted methods of keeping in touch with parents are not equally successful. Sometimes it is enough to keep parents informed via phone calls, notes sent home, or school or district websites. When using a school website to convey information, it is also good practice to add a link to the district website to direct parents there to review policies or other districtwide issues.

Administrators should help parents (with teacher involvement) in creating a rubric to monitor and adjust accordingly their attitude toward correcting a child's behavior in classrooms. Parents should include a checklist and rubric for the examination of homework and a positive weekly communication with the child's teachers and administrators. A tool that has proven to be very successful, particularly at the middle school and junior high levels, is the student planner or agenda booklet. Administrators and teachers who encourage parents to check the agendas on a daily basis will find that students are more organized and more apt to do their assignments—and on time!

Schools should look into Internet programs such as Blackboard or SchoolNotes to post announcements, homework assignments, upcoming projects, schedules, and events. Moreover, once the programs are up and running, we must make certain that the parents are aware of their existence and are given ample instruction on how to utilize them to the best possible extent.

Access to all of the web-based tools in the world, all of the backpack letters, and all of the student agendas does not guarantee that parents are going to monitor their children's school life and responsibilities. Administrators must gain the respect and support of their faculty to work together to lead parents to take responsibility for and interest in the instruction of their children.

Attendance is another important part and therefore certainly should not be overlooked when discussing classroom management and parental involvement. It is a parent's responsibility, as well as law, that students miss as little instruction as possible. Certainly, there are days when students are not feeling well or when personal emergencies prevent a child from attending school. However, repeated unexcused absences not only affect the child's ability to keep up with expected lessons but also build an atmosphere where students are not motivated to participate when they are present.

Schools and school districts have many options for holding parents accountable and inspiring new incentives for parents regarding attendance issues. Legislating that parents be held accountable may be a forcible solution in assuring that children get the required education. District-level administrators might devise a variety of consequences for students with excessive absences. For example, one might lose academic credit, receive a failing grade for a grading quarter, be remanded to in-school or out-of-school suspension, be required to attend Saturday or other alternative schooling, or be subjected to prosecution. Some states hold parents accountable for student absences, imposing fines or other court-directed actions.

Perhaps schools might have to work on an individual basis with parents who do not stand behind the requirements that students attend school regularly. In order to achieve this, the school must first determine the actual reason for the excessive absences. There may be many factors that prevent a student from regularly attending school. Although some of these factors do not condone absences, they at least give us a point of reference—a place where we can begin to understand and work with the families to increase attendance. Following are some issues we might have to consider:

- Do the parents work long shifts or hold more than one job, making it a necessity for the student to assume some of the duties for running the household?
- Are the parents new to this country and perhaps not used to our system?
- Are the students too tired to come to school?
- Do their responsibilities include caring for younger siblings, thereby interfering with the school schedule of the older child?
- Is the student expected to maintain employment to help support the family?
- Is there a family unit with which the child resides?
- Is there communication between the student and the parent or guardian?
- Are the parents aware that the student does not attend school?
- Is the child afraid to come to school for fear of being bullied?
- Does the student fear the work expected of him at school?

Once we have identified the reason a student has excessive absences, regardless of whether this is a contributing factor to overall classroom participation or behavior, we can then move on to resolving the problem. Part of a successful classroom management plan is to get to know your students. One need not move in with a student, nor is it necessary to make frequent home visits, to uncover the home situation. Successful teachers listen to students, give them an outlet to talk over their concerns, provide encouragement, and let students know that there are adults who care and are genuinely interested.

Once the teacher has a fairly good picture of the outside forces that affect the student, specifically as related to her roles with her parents or guardians, the administrator steps in to lend assistance. Administrators have the means to begin programs that can deal with some of the situations we have just posed. The magnitude of the programs is dictated by the number of students who have excessive absences—or are constantly tardy—as well as students who may attend school on a relatively regular basis but who might have similar home lives as the students who have raised our radars.

Programs that involve students, parents, and schools vary to accommodate the needs of the school community. The successful administrator not only looks for inside resources to address these issues but also opens the program to the entire community. Day-care centers can be opened on or near secondary school property. The older children can assist in the care of these young clients, either as part of the curriculum or by creating paid positions.

By using high school students to help run the day-care centers, the operating costs could be lower than for other facilities. The lower cost might in turn help the financially struggling parents. With the younger children now under directed care, the normally absent student would be relieved of having the responsibility of being the caretaker of her younger siblings.

Schools that already have such a program in place offer an opportunity to the parents, the children being attended to, and the

high school students doing the job. The parents are assured that
their children are in capable hands, are in a safe environment, and
are supervised.

The young children benefit from the opportunity to interact
with children of their own age as well as the older student chaper-
ones. Since they are already in a school setting, it is easy to inter-
twine academic activities with playtime. The older students not
only learn about child care from a parental perspective but also,
when serving as tutors, gain a better insight to the world as seen
through the eyes of educators.

Unpaid positions where students gain academic credit are even
less burdened by overhead, and children could receive care with
no cost to the parents while the older children prepare for a career
in child care. Perhaps an even more beneficial gain of running an
in-school day care is that the students who act as teachers or
guardians for the young ones graduate from high school much better equipped than their nonparticipating peers to be responsible
and successful parents.

Too often we are willing to encourage parents to play a major
role in the academic lives of their elementary school children.
However, as the children grow up we tend to back away from seeking support and interest from parents. Perhaps this is because as
we see these young students grow, we understand that in addition
to the scholarly information we pass on to them, we must instill in
them a sense of maturity, responsibility, and independence. Unfortunately it would seem that parents are of the same mind-set.

We believe that Americans are not capable of making informed
decisions about whom to vote for until they are eighteen years old.
Why then should we assume that before the age of eighteen these
same citizens are ready to take responsibility for the choices they
make for their own lives? Minors need the help and direction of
adults—family as well as educators. Parents and educators should
realize the need to continue to keep the lines of communication
open between school, student, and home, all the way through high

school graduation. Parents' input regarding the choices for high school classes are as important as their input in the discipline and overall classroom management plan as regards their children. This is not to say that we should encourage parents not to trust their older school-aged children. The message we want to convey is that all students from preschool through graduation need to know that they have adults that care about them and to whom they can turn for words of encouragement and guidance. Parents cannot guess what goes on during the school day. Therefore, it is up to the educators to ensure that parents get the word, be it via letters, phone calls, e-mails, websites, meetings, student planners, or even a well-placed message board outside of the school building.

The main focus of educational policy has been on institutional reforms within schools: in teaching practices, curriculum modifications, organizational changes, or conventional privatization reforms (school choice or vouchers). Almost all these policy reforms recognize that families do play an influential role in the success of students.

Advocates of NCLB argue that school choice, among other benefits, energizes parents to become more involved in the education of their children. But the issue is one of proportion. The substance of parental involvement has been marginal relative to the possibilities represented by families for improving the education of their children. Rather, school policy for improving educational outcomes has been far more preoccupied with pressuring schools to change than with inducing change in families.

One way to observe this emphasis is to compare the formal restrictions placed on schools with those placed on families. The schools that our children attend are subject to a sheaf of laws, rules, regulations, directives, guidelines, and policies that are far too extensive for enumeration.

In contrast, the formal requirement for family participation in education as embodied in law is trivial. Basically, there is a single requirement: A child must meet compulsory attendance requirements (or meet participation requirements as set out for home schooling). But if better educational results are to be achieved, it is obvious that schools cannot do it alone. Changes in family behavior will be necessary as well. Of course, families are not the property of the state, whereas schools, more easily regulated, are public agencies. At issue is how to induce families to make these changes.

A wealth of literature exists documenting the strong ties between a family's socioeconomic status (SES) and children's educational performance. SES is an important indicator we can use to monitor children's cognitive growth and overall success as students. When considering SES to help us understand student growth, we must look at a student's home life, activities in which he engages that are not part of school, and the quality and quantity of parental involvement.

Studies show that families with high SES tend to produce children who are successful students. One reason is because these families often have a parent who does not work and is home to tend to the needs of the children. Additionally, families with high SES tend to be holders of college degrees and understand the need to pass that value on to their children. And, these parents are the most likely to maintain the structure of school life in the home.

However, this idea can be replicated with families who do not have high SES. Schools should work with these parents to ensure that they have set aside specific times for students to do homework as a normal part of their daily routine.

To whatever extent possible, the homework area should be free of distraction. On hand should be a parent, other adult, or older sibling to assist the child as needed. This tutor figure should sit with the child during the entire homework process. Also at hand should be supplies, books, computers, and other resources the child might need to complete the homework.

When we notice that a parent would like to assist her child but that the home atmosphere might not be conducive to positive learning, perhaps it might be suggested that the parent or guardian accompany the child to the local library. The environment is not only suitable for study but also offers a wealth of resources and trained individuals to lend assistance.

Parents from high SES families maintain higher paying jobs than families with low SES. Their English language skills tend to be stronger and their literacy skills higher. Once more, schools or school districts do have the ability to assist low SES families by offering free or inexpensive lessons for the parents. Such sessions would include English for speakers of other languages (ESOL), reading, and tips on how to tutor their children. Schools or school districts can set up such programs but might look to volunteers from families with high SES to assist with the running of the programs.

Finally, families with high SES are apt to provide their children with ample nutritious food. Free or inexpensive nutritious snacks should be made available at the school for students from low SES families who opt to come to school before or after hours for extra assistance. If parents of low SES are taking their children to the local library to do homework, schools can work with the library to set up a separate section for "homework students," and the snacks can be waiting for them there.

Perhaps in these cases, the schools or districts can turn to the high SES families to seek donations of either healthy snacks or funds to purchase them. Students who do not have to concentrate on the fact that they are hungry have time to concentrate on their studies. Students who are malnourished are ill-equipped to become successful learners.

Children from high SES families generally are more apt to have strong social ties. They often reside in one home for longer periods of time wherein they can establish close community ties. The social lives of these children are usually well structured in that they are likely to be members of local teams and social organizations. Schools often overlook this aspect of a student's life when considering classroom management programs. However, this is not an area that the school should ignore. If we expect structure and dedication from our students in the classroom, they must have examples to follow throughout their entire lives, not just from 8:00 a.m. to 3:00 p.m., Monday through Friday.

Most school districts have some sort of social or athletic program already in place. But, how many involve the parents? Parental involvement is important for many reasons, not the least of which is to build a positive relationship between the parent and the child as well as the parent and the school. For example, why should school music programs ignore parental involvement? Certainly some of the parents are musically talented in one way or another.

Schools often hold athletic events at which students compete against faculty. Why not extend the invitation to parents? Those who are not athletically inclined might join in by assisting in some of the administrative and logistic chores of the event. Could bilingual parents serve as interpreters for parents that are reluctant to attend school programs because they feel their lack of English gets in the way?

Children who grow up in high SES families are often afforded culturally rich opportunities that children from low SES families might not enjoy. Many schools, particularly in large urban areas, have implemented programs to fill in where the parents are unable. There are dance programs for students that are conducted after school by school staff. There are a multitude of field trips to local museums, or for city children, to zoos, petting parks, farms, or trips out into the country.

However, more can and arguably should be done to help enrich these students. Schools might invite guests to talk and work with students in their own schools. These guests might come from nearby museums, park services, or trade schools such as schools for fine arts, or perhaps they might be renowned people who might reside in or near the school district.

High SES families usually have the means to select choice daycare facilities to enrich their children's education versus a babysitting service or, worse, leaving the children to fend for themselves. As we already mentioned, high schools can offer free or reduced-cost day-care centers on the high school grounds. Families should be made aware that these programs exist and should be strongly encouraged to enroll their children. Communication, particularly in languages other than English where applicable, is paramount to the success of these types of programs.

In addition to programs that are available during regular school months, schools can work with the community to identify means of offering enrichment programs to students over the summer months. High SES families might be using this time to take their children to other cities or countries, whereas low SES families are more likely to remain in town. Summer enrichment programs can bring a little of the culture these students are missing to them in their own setting. Art and music appreciation and awareness programs and international history, culture, and cuisine are just a few of the items that top the list of possibilities.

Schools might look to family members as well as the resources found in the entire community to help present workshops or classes. Parents or other community members undoubtedly have experiences that they can share about these cultural topics should the school district find it difficult to identify funds for such programs.

Parents of low SES status should be explored as a tool for the success of summer programs. While many of these parents might not be available for weeks at a time, some might be able to give up a day off from work to teach a craft from their country of origin, conduct a folklore storytelling session, demonstrate ethnic cooking, or present a show-and-tell type session to teach children about artwork from other cultures. Some parents might be willing to conduct introductory language classes with students who do not speak these languages.

Language barriers, lack of transportation, insufficient education, or the inability to leave work for any amount of time are just some of the factors that keep low SES parents from being active participants in their children's education. Schools can facilitate access for these parents by providing adequate communication, particularly in languages other than English, as needed.

The key to success, however, is to make the effort to involve the parents. If left out of the loop, parents who have limited resources such as the use of the Internet are less apt to know about issues and activities in their children's education. Alternate resources to bring these families in are out there. It is up to the level you establish of community involvement, positive interpersonal skills, insightfulness, and flexibility of the school staff whether success is achieved.

If schools are to reach the required adequate yearly progress (AYP) as set by the NCLB guidelines, a concentrated effort must be made to bring up test scores of students who come from low SES families. An important tool to achieve this is by involving the parents. This task should not be overly taxing or unattainable if we just exercise a few essential steps:

- Properly use successful leadership skills.
- Practice good, solid managerial competency.
- Make use of all available resources in the community.
- Keep abreast of successful programs already in place around the country.

At times it might seem as if the relationship between our schools or districts and the parents of our students is unique—unlike any other district in the country. However, we are not alone. Undoubtedly there are districts or individual schools that look very much like our own. The key is to find them, identify how they keep in touch with parents, and examine their success stories. Doing this is not as difficult a task as it might appear. Now is when we turn to the Internet.

Let us not forget that the Internet provides us with an almost unlimited source of information. You can easily visit websites of schools around the nation to learn about programs they have in place and the success rate of each. Once you locate a program that seems to fit the needs of your school community, do not be afraid to contact leaders from these schools, via e-mail or telephone, to ask questions about program success and perhaps how to tailor such programs to fit the needs of your school or district.

Successful school districts recognize the need to connect with parents, and many have put into motion programs designed to assist parents in becoming part of their children's educational process. They make their actions public via the scores of websites that explain specific parent–student–school models. If your district does not have such a website, you might wish to suggest that one be created. Examples can be seen by researching websites of individual school districts or by searching central data banks such as those provided by the U.S. Department of Education.

Use all available resources—including colleagues from your own building—to identify specific practices and opportunities that parents from both high and low SES families can employ to improve educational outcomes. Form a task force to research what other schools have done, then put together a plan to unite the school and parent and ultimately to follow the plan through.

Another action that enables school districts, parents, and students to work together to improve academic achievement and behavioral issues is a result of the New York State Education Department's Regent shared decision-making policy. This policy ensures that a child's parents (or guardians, grandparents, or any other person who is legally responsible) are a part of the decision-making process.

All New York school districts are required to develop a plan that will allow parents, administrators, and board members to participate in decisions made by the individual school buildings. Each building must create a site-based management team to review academic procedures, social events, and class management issues.

There are a multitude of polls, surveys, and other research that tell us conflicting information about how parents view their roles with schools. Some proclaim that parents are satisfied with the job teachers are doing and that they feel secure knowing that their children are in safe, nurturing learning environments all day. Others indicate that parents believe schools are not doing enough. Often we find parents willing to help with their children's education; more often we find parents who are not willing or able. Finally, sometimes we find schools are reluctant to elicit too much involvement of parents. It is up to each school or district—as an entire community—to determine the type of school and parent relationship that works best for them.

If you are to bring parents on board, you must be certain that the parents are well informed regarding school issues. The parents must be committed to be a part of the team. The following checklist may bring about an understanding of how to establish that working relationship between the parent and teacher.

Checklist for Parents

_____ I know the names of all of my child's teachers and how to contact them.

_____ I know where to check for homework and upcoming tests or assignments.

_____ I check my child's planner each night for assignments and messages.

_____ I know the students' rights and responsibilities and support them at home.

_____ I know the dress code and ensure that my child does not violate it.

_____ I have prepared a list of concerns the teachers should know about my child.

_____ I have volunteered for at least one task at my child's school.

_____ I check the school website for news updates.

_____ I introduced myself to the teachers on Back to School Night.

_____ I ask my child for his or her comments on each class every evening.

_____ I have provided an area that can assist my child in doing his or her homework.

4

THE INVOLVEMENT
OF THE COMMUNITY

The value of community involvement in schools can be traced back to at least the early nineteenth century. At that time, the large German immigrant community played a supportive role for administrators by helping initiate a new curriculum, such as drawing, singing, and vocational classes. Their input also included the introduction of learning a second language, specifically German. This initiative became the model that prompted public schools to include introduction of other languages and bilingual programs. The incentive was to attempt to attract middle-class students from private and boarding schools, but the result became common practice in today's schools. The Germans also contributed to the overall structure of the school regarding behavioral concerns of the teaching staff.

The validation for this limited power was already developed through their cultural accomplishments in science, art, and literature. While German community influences focused on curriculum and were quite successful, not all groups were as politically adept and could claim the same. For example, throughout the formation of our public school system, certain ethnic groups—such as Asians and Blacks—fell victim to discrimination. Segregation and other acts against these groups resulted in a large gap in academic success. Although these practices of inequality have lessened or disappeared, some ethnic groups remain victims of history. Academic achievement remains low. Often students become members of gangs. Positive contribution to the community is lacking.

A particular reformation act in Atlanta at the end of the nineteenth century illustrates the positive effect of the community on classroom management. The driving issue in this case was that of corporal punishment. The situation was so severe that the mayor of Atlanta felt it necessary to remove his children from public schools, and he became the advocate to abolish this type of behavior.

Before success was attained, there was a setback that is based on community involvement. The media had reported on certain incidents of child abuse in the schools. One particular story told of a child who was severely beaten by a teacher after allegedly pulling out a knife in the classroom. A grievance committee found in favor of the teacher, and the measure to abolish corporal punishment throughout the district was defeated by the board twelve to four. The committee's argument was that schools were not disciplining students as harshly as they could.

However, the day after the vote to keep corporal punishment, the city council abolished the school board, and one of the first actions of the newly appointed board was to incorporate a prohibition on corporal punishment in the district.

When looking at the overall school community, we include the school, the families of our students, the business community, and all those in the private sector surrounding the school district. The key words we must keep in mind when talking about community are involvement and information. Communities cannot be expected to become involved in an activity if they are not well informed of its existence or its mission. The task of communication is a two-way effort. Schools must communicate with the community, and the community must have an avenue through which they can access the schools.

There are several ways a school can interact with the entire community. Many schools across the nation are using a variety of means that have proven to be most successful. These schools are advocates of the notion that if parents are well informed of what is happening with their children, they are more apt to get involved in the education process and along the way encourage the aid of their colleagues who make up the extended school community.

We agree with this concept and offer here examples of how some schools around the country successfully keep both parents and community informed.

Weekly letters sent home with elementary school children is one method that is widely used and is very successful. These letters may contain more information on some weeks than on others. Nevertheless, by sending letters home every week, students begin to develop a habit that is in fact building their sense of responsibility, thereby reducing the amount of information that never makes it home. In addition to the skills the students develop, sending messages home on a regularly scheduled basis helps parents become a part of their children's school community.

Parents also soon come to expect them. These weekly letters can include information concerning classroom activities, schoolwide activities, upcoming events, notification of changes at school, requests for volunteer assistance, dates of early dismissal or school closings, or any other information that would allow a parent to feel part of his child's learning environment.

While we have seen much success in the level of communication between school and family via such letters, we must also consider how such correspondence is beneficial to our relationship with the entire community. For example, when teachers assign research projects, a copy of the requirements and rubric should be sent to local libraries to assist their reference personnel as they attempt to guide our students.

Many schools send a list of required materials to local stores, especially in the summer, just before the opening of school. By doing so, it becomes easier for parents to know what supplies to buy for their students, eliminating the diversion of academic time to discussion of logistics in the classroom. Students who come to class with the proper supplies are apt to be more focused on the lesson than on trying to pull together a clean sheet of paper and a pencil to take notes.

Elimination of this distraction helps the teacher keep the class on task, contributing to the success of the classroom management program. Finally, letting local stores know what students will be looking to purchase helps the stores in a couple of ways. It gives them advance notice of the items they should have on hand. It also gives them an idea of what is going on in the schools. Let us imagine that a particular middle school requires their students to start the school year by bringing in to their science class packets of seeds, little gardening tools, tiny planters, and so on. If the school sends the required supply list to the local nurseries, when the students arrive to purchase their items, the nursery might be ready not only with the items but also with additional reading material.

Perhaps the manager or owner could come to the class as a guest speaker. The students would benefit from learning from someone actually in the field. The nursery has a stake in this endeavor as well since the students are approaching the age where they will be looking for a part-time or summer job. If they are exposed to the types of things that go on at the nursery, perhaps they would be interested in seeking employment there, which helps the nursery locate interested potential employees. Additionally beneficial to the nursery is the notion that these students get their first exposure to the training they might need at the nursery from an actual nursery employee.

Electronic messages can be used in areas where it is certain that a great majority of parents have access to computers on a daily basis. When gathering emergency contact information at the beginning of the school year, parents should include their home and/or work e-mail addresses. Schools, grade levels, teams, departments, or individual classes can create a mailing list so that all parents can receive e-mail information with one click of the send button. In areas where the demographics suggest that the vast majority of parents do not have access to the Internet, a concentrated effort must be made to find a method to distribute information to everyone via the traditional paper messages.

Messages have to reach the entire parent population, not just in the physical sense but also in the sense that the messages have to be understood by the parents. Once more, demographics play an important role in determining what language to use for the messages. It might be that in order to get your message across to the majority of the parents, a school might have to send home messages in Spanish, Italian, Polish, Farsi, Korean, or whatever is the predominant language in that area.

If the school or district does not have the means to hire someone to translate weekly correspondence into one or more of these languages, it might try looking to the community to set up a bank of volunteers to handle this task. This not only gets the job done but also opens new avenues to reach parents and the community. Seeking out parents to serve as volunteers ensures that their participation keeps them abreast of the goings-on in the school, and it also makes them a true part of the school community.

Social and business relationships most likely exist among parents with similar cultural or ethnic backgrounds. These groups can serve to expand your pool of resources for translating tasks as well as provide any other talents they may be able to bring to the table. Once parents are assured that there will be colleagues present at school functions who understand not only their language but also their customs, they will feel more comfortable attending school functions, participating in meetings with teachers, and lending assistance to the school wherever needed.

By maintaining constant contact with these groups, the individuals concerned are apt to share information about similar interests and skills. As they learn about the school or district and identify needs that they can fill for the school, they are likely to take interest. Increased knowledge and interest encourages and brings forth a feeling of community. The outcome will inevitably be a growth in the volunteer bank, not just of people but also of the resources they bring with them. Ask the bank of language volunteers to attend parent–teacher meetings and act as translators.

As we continue to examine possible examples of community involvement, let us take a moment to reflect on our story about Ricky and the situation involving the boys he sat with in the cafeteria. These boys normally hang around the parking lot at the local shopping center and were seen as problem students in the past. Although the schools may not have a legal say in the activities at local shopping centers, it is in the best interest of the school, the students, the parents, and the neighborhood as a whole to look after the children in their area during nonclass hours. This is an example of when one might wish to take the whole-tribe approach to raising a child.

There may be little or no legal obligation, but there is a moral obligation for the community to do whatever possible to ensure that neighborhood students are safe and cared for properly.

At the school Ricky attends, the administrators and the managers at the shopping center would have to work together to devise a plan that would deter the boys from becoming a nuisance. An after-school program that engages them in both academic and fun activities would give the boys a place to go until their parents return home from work. The owners of the businesses in the shopping center might be willing to donate equipment, snacks, or funds to assist the school in running an after-school program.

Schools could seek venues in the community that offer activities for children. Through a business partnership program, for example, plans could be devised that provide the children with a safe environment that is also an adult-supervised place to go at the end of the school day. Parents must be made aware of these choices and encouraged to persuade their children to attend.

Such choices might include the following activities that could be directed to begin as soon as the students demonstrate that they have completed the homework assignments for that day. The adults at the venues that provide the following activities would also serve as mentors to oversee the completion of homework before beginning the fun activities.

- Swim teams could be formed at the community pool.
- At the public library, students can listen to stories read to them or can watch videos, listen to music, or become engaged in supervised computer activities.
- The school could launch a major campaign to support intramural sports programs such as traveling leagues.
- Local movie theaters, working as business partners with the school, could offer age-appropriate movies at a greatly reduced price. Perhaps they could set aside specific low-volume patron times, such as directly after school, and show G, PG, and/or PG-13 movies. This arrangement would not only give latchkey students a place to go but also allow the local theaters to benefit from the extra revenue. After feeling like true members of the school's overall community, perhaps the managers could be persuaded to let the school use the theater as a venue for certain school events.
- Older students can become involved with local police and fire departments to work together and possibly build career skills. There are several of these types of activities already offered around the country. For example, the Search and Rescue Explorer Program of Huntington Beach, California, is one such program that has proven to be quite successful.
- Cooperation with places of worship, community centers, and other such venues can also provide programs to keep children engaged in supervised activities between the hours that they leave school and when their parents return home from work.

There are programs that promote interaction between the schools and the rest of the community. A visit to the websites of school districts helps provide you with ideas of the programs offered around the country. Although this may seem like searching for a needle in a haystack, the task is not impossible. We have found Internet search engines, such as google.com, to be excellent resources when researching matters pertaining to school activities.

We realize that it is practically impossible to know the names of all schools and districts in the country. However, we also found that by searching the names of U.S. presidents or other prominent figures in U.S. history or literature, we identified a vast number of websites for schools or districts.

Some of the activities provided by schools are sports, music, drama, and other such traditional clubs. Schools attempt to maintain good attendance in these activities by promoting them as rewards for good behavior. A display of unacceptable behavior or declining grades could result in prohibiting the student from continued participation until the problem is rectified.

Many districts are turning to another form of after-school programming that provides both academic and fun activities and involves the local community. The program targets older students—middle to high school—rather than many of the similar programs that provide care for younger children.

For these alternative programs, students can participate on their own volition, by request of the parents, or by recommendation of a school official. Usually the school recommendation is based on the student's behavioral history. For example, if a student has served repeated detentions or has been suspended (in or out of school) several times, the administrators might deem that participation in this program is a worthwhile next step to deter continued unacceptable behavior.

Generally, school sites house the programs, which begin at the end of the school day and end at an agreed upon (by school and parental consensus) set time. A typical setting for this program is one in which the students work on homework or other school assignments for a set amount of time, usually about an hour, and then engage in a variety of fun activities. Some programs include snacks for the students during this time.

Teachers (paid or volunteer), volunteers from the overall community, or a combination of both can staff the homework portion of the program. Funds to pay teachers or other supervisors might be obtained through a grant. The number and type of members of the volunteer bank depend on the community. For the nonacademic portion of the program, schools tend to rely on volunteers from the community. Some sources of volunteers might be parents, residents of local retirement villages, business partners, or student leaders from the local high schools.

To ensure a successful classroom management program that extends beyond normal school hours, the collaboration of various community members and educators is essential. Teams made up of representatives of the entire community bring a wealth of knowledge and resources to enhance a student's learning experiences. One direction is to add to the students' education, and another includes preparing students for life after graduation.

Many districts use community medical organizations to provide assistance. In some cases medical personnel, such as nurses, help students learn a trade as well as help them develop their work ethic. This close affiliation with community businesses and organizations tends to help both college-bound and non-college-bound students decide what field they might pursue after graduation. There are character education lessons to be learned as the students begin to work with the public and gain an understanding of maintaining a successful business.

Both students and businesses should benefit from such work–study programs. State regulations are set to prevent businesses from hiring students before legal age, to limit the amount of hours a student works, and to ensure that students are attending and passing classes at school while engaged in the work–study program.

Teachers who oversee these programs meet regularly with their students to review their work experiences and to monitor academic success.

Many businesses are willing to work around school schedules to employ students, and still more are willing to provide jobs for younger teens. Small businesses that are willing to open doors for young teens often help these youngsters build self-esteem and a sense of responsibility during their formative years.

Good academic and behavioral skills should be learned in the classroom and the business place and should be practiced equally in both. There are a variety of excellent programs that build and emphasize these traits. One such program is the "school to career" model, where students shadow people in the workforce to gain knowledge of the business as well as the work ethic. For example, students see firsthand the importance of punctuality, low absenteeism, honesty, team effort, and cooperation. In another program, Cooperative Work Experience, a student has the opportunity to select a business that might lead to a career path.

Neither of these, nor any of the other successful programs, puts the job before the school. In each case, students must maintain passing grades in their school subjects, show continued good attendance, and be free of serious offenses that result in suspensions—either in or out of school. The employers play an important role in aiding the students. They are the role models. They must instill the work ethic as well as the importance of maintaining good academic skills in the minds of these students.

Programs such as these are win–win situations for all parties involved. Some of the task of character education is moved from the schools to the businesses. Businesses get a firsthand look at potential future employees. Students learn about life experiences. To ensure the success of these work–study programs, schools must establish a regular collaboration between school and business by monitoring student progress and showing support for the businesses. Schools need to ensure that students are benefiting from the program, and the businesses must realize that they have the support of the schools.

Certain agreements should be established on how to address a variety of situations that might arise. For example, if a student has problems in school that result in suspension, the business should agree to not allow her to work during the suspension period. If the student has to serve detention, he must realize the possible consequences he might encounter at his place of employment. If grades slip, students can be forced to cut back on the amount of hours on the job. Naturally, these interruptions can be quite harmful to local businesses.

Therefore, it becomes very necessary to establish a strong collaboration between job and school. Both parties are responsible for ensuring that the students learn the importance of responsible behavior both on the job and at school. Many work–study programs fail to maintain acceptable academic achievement and good work ethic primarily because there is no strong and constantly open line of communication between the place of business and the school.

Once more, the role of the parent cannot be overlooked. Parents are the community members who have, or should have, the closest relationship with the students. It is the responsibility of the parents to cooperate with the rules of the work–study programs. The lines of communication between school and parent must also remain constantly open to achieve success.

Even in cases where a particular parent might not be the best role model for her child, there is hope. Perhaps the family situation is such that the income provided by the child is more important to the family unit than is the student's GPA. Here the need for schools to maintain a solid effort to keep the parent advised of the benefits of the program is crucial.

The school must elicit the assistance of the parent to monitor the student's progress at school and on the job, at the same time demonstrating to the parent that the student will be getting the utmost support of the school. Once again, in cases such as these, educators must truly take seriously the role of in loco parentis.

Programs with community businesses such as technology labs, photo shops, colleges, universities, and local businesses all help to benefit student learning. For example, a school in the Southwest that was in dire need of repair reached out to the community for assistance. The principal of the school and all of its employees (e.g., social workers, custodians) knocked on the doors of residents and invited families and businesspeople to join in a discussion as to what they wanted in the way of a new school. One citizen who owned a small business gave assistance by helping with the manual labor of the new construction, and yet another offered a donation of some of the supplies.

In other communities similar events and collaborations take place. Businesses are a great source of well-needed funds, but we must not forget that they are staffed with humans who have a variety of skills. Perhaps a student in a particular district has a parent or guardian who is a licensed electrician and can donate a few hours to help with related needs. Repainting can be rather costly, but if a local paint store is willing to donate a few gallons of paint, high school students and parents might provide the manpower to give a school a new look.

Community involvement is such that school administrators must seek outside help and maintain good relations with all public community groups to resist the pressure of criticism directed at schools. Groups such as civic organizations (Lions, Kiwanis, Rotary, Jaycees), cultural groups (literary, art, music, architecture, drama), intercultural education and race relations, economic (labor unions, chambers of commerce, real estate boards, retail merchants associations), government (local, state, county), recreation, law enforcement, safety, family life, child care, and housing all need to take part.

Religious organizations provide moral and spiritual values in the community. Likewise, political groups that are involved with such issues as voting and registration can influence what goes on in our educational environment. Both types of organizations direct their programs with the goal of enhancing overall school operation and maintaining a solid relationship. Such alliances between these groups and the schools make a difference in how some students behave and function in school. Just a few of the community organizations that promote positive social and behavioral practices, such as good sportsmanship and anger management, follow:

- The local health department or hospitals, with programs such as candy stripers or student aides
- Recreation departments
- Retirement groups
- Youth organizations such as the YMCA, YWCA, and Hebrew organizations

Maintaining good relations with all these groups is beneficial to administrators, teachers, and parents while seeking out resources for troubled youth or keeping good students on track.

Administrators who maintain a close and positive relationship with the local business community are successful. Valuable resources for both parties are identified. Students, parents, and educators are brought closer. The result is a win–win situation for everyone.

CONCLUSION

At the beginning of this book, we asked how one would go about turning an ineffective classroom management plan around. How would we, as members of the entire educational community, improve classroom behavior? What can we do to enhance the overall learning environment? How can we ensure that students are afforded the best possible opportunity to learn? We asked how teachers can effectively work with parents to ensure students receive an optimal learning experience.

To answer those questions, we defined the essential roles of the entire community in the process of formulating a successful classroom management plan. Our examples are of effective skills we as leaders in administration, in our classrooms, in our families, and in our communities should use to ensure that students grow both academically and as successful members of society.

We provided guidelines for administrators so that they might assist teachers with classroom management. We outlined specific ideas for teachers, parents, and the community to use to work together. We offered self-assessment tools for teachers, administrators, and parents. There are several websites listed in the further resources section to help direct readers to follow up on the information provided in each chapter of this book.

The next step is up to the readers. Now is the time to reflect upon classroom management and examine what our roles have been. More important, it is time to plan what our roles will be. Keeping in mind that classroom management means more than just controlling misbehavior, we can focus on the other components of a successful classroom management plan. It is time to ask ourselves some essential questions:

- Are our classrooms, buildings, and grounds set up for a positive and safe learning environment?
- Are our rules clearly defined and accepted by educators, parents, and students?
- Do teachers have the support and resources to continue honing their skills?
- What programs are in place to assist students outside of the normal school day? What can we add?
- Is our entire community being utilized to the fullest extent possible?
- What other resources are available, and how do we go about getting them?

The intention of this book is to demonstrate how a successful classroom management plan should look, how to examine the plans already in practice, and how to identify what we need to do to the existing plans to bring them from good to great. By separating the book into four different chapters—teachers, administrators, parents, and the local community—we segregated several issues pertaining to each group and gave them the resources necessary to enhance student learning. However, this was not an easy task, as we are sure you have grown to appreciate as you read through the pages. It is virtually impossible to completely separate the groups. No classroom management plan can be truly successful if one of these components is left out or not used to its fullest potential.

The rest is up to you. We have provided the tools; it is your turn to use them. All children deserve the best possible opportunity to make the best of their lives. Laws see that educators do their part. We have a civic duty to teach our children well—to build strong minds and strong moral fortitude.

REFERENCES AND FURTHER RESOURCES

REFERENCES

Bloom, B. S. (1976). *Human Characteristics and School Learning.* New York: McGraw-Hill.

Bloom, B. S. (1981). *All Our Children Learning: A Primer for Parents, Teachers, and Other Educators.* New York: McGraw-Hill.

Charter School of Excellence. (2003). Parent Contract. Retrieved December 2006 from www.charterschool.com/ParentContract.asp.

Coleman, J. S. (1966). The 1966 Study on Equality of Educational Opportunity. Retrieved May 29, 2007, from http://www.eb.com:180/cgi-bin/g?DocF=micro/702/16.html

Glickman, C. (2002). *Leadership for Learning.* Alexandria, VA: Association for Supervision and Curriculum Development.

Hopkins, G. (2003). Classroom Management: Principals Help Teachers Develop Essential Skills. Retrieved September 28, 2005, from www.education-world.com.

Ingersoll, R. (2002, June). The Teacher Shortage: A Case of Wrong Diagnosis and Wrong Prescription. *NASSP Bulletin,* 16–31.

Kohn, M. L. (1969). *Class and Conformity: A Study in Values.* Homewood, IL: Dorsey Press.

Langley, N., & Jacobs, M. (2006). *Five Essential Skills for School Leaders: Moving from Good to Great.* Lanham, MD: Rowman & Littlefield Education.

MacLeod, J. (1995). *Ain't No Makin' It.* Boulder, CO: Westview.

Marzano, R. (2001). *Classroom Instruction That Works.* Alexandria, VA: ASCD.

Read, A. W. (1996). *The New International Webster's Comprehensive Dictionary of the English Language: Deluxe Encyclopedic Edition.* Naples, FL: Trident Press International.

Snow, C. E., Barnes, W. S., Chandler, J., Goodman, I. F., & Hemphill, L. (1991). *Unfulfilled Expectations: Home and School Influences on Literacy.* Cambridge, MA: Harvard University Press.

Stacy, T. W., & Gold, D. A. (2005). *You Can't Scare Me . . . I Have a Teenager.* Washington, DC: Child and Family Press.

"Talk to Teachers before Sending the Disruptive Students Back to Class." (2006). *American Educator, 30*(2).

Tharpe, R. G., & Gallimore, R. (1992). *Rousing Minds to Life: Teaching, Learning, and Schooling in Social Context.* New York: Press Syndicate of the University of Cambridge.

Tomlinson, C. A. (1999). *The Differentiated Classroom: Responding to the Needs of All Learners.* Alexandria, Virginia. ASCD.

U.S. Department of Education, Office for Civil Rights. (2000). *Elementary and Secondary School Civil Rights Compliance Report.* Columbus, OH: National Coalition to Abolish Corporal Punishment in Schools.

FURTHER RESOURCES

Bagin, D., Gallagher, D. R., & Kindred, L. W. (1994). *The School and Community Relations.* Needham Heights, MA: Allyn & Bacon.

Canter, L. (2001). *Assertive Discipline: Positive Behavior Management for Today's Classroom.* Los Angeles: Canter & Associates.

Canter, L. (2002). *Responsible Behavior Curriculum Guide.* Los Angeles: Canter & Associates.

Christensen, S., & Rosen, A. (1999). The Family Connection of St. Joseph County, Inc. for Partners in Learning. *Indiana Center for Family, School & Community Partnerships Newsletter, 2,* 2.

Dodd, A. W., & Konzal, J. L. (2002). *How Communities Build Stronger Schools*. New York: Palgrave Macmillan.

Dewey, J., & Archambault, R. D. (1964). *John Dewey on Education; Selected Writings*. New York: Modern Library.

DuFour, R., & Eaker, R. (1998). *Professional Learning Communities at Work*. Alexandria, VA: Association for Supervision and Curriculum Development.

Esquith, R. (2003). *There Are No Shortcuts*. New York: Pantheon.

Grossman, H. (2004). *Classroom Behavior Management for Diverse and Inclusive Schools*. Lanham, MD: Rowman & Littlefield Education.

Jones, F. H. (2003). More Time on Task, Less Goofing Off. Retrieved August 2003 from www.educationworld.com

Levin, H. M., & Belfield, C. (2003). A Contract for Families. *American School Board Journal, 190*, 29–32.

Levinson, B. A. U., Borman, K. M., Eisenhart, M., Foster, M., Fox, A. E., & Sutton, M. (2000). *Schooling the Symbolic Animal*. Lanham, MD: Rowman & Littlefield Education.

Lindberg, J., Kelley, D., & Swick, A. (2005). *Common-Sense Classroom Management for Middle and High School Teachers*. Thousand Oaks, CA: Corwin.

Johnson, S. (2005). *Everything Bad Is Good for You*. New York: Penguin.

Marzano, R. (2003). *What Works in Schools: Translating Research into Action*. Alexandria, VA: Association for Supervision and Curriculum Development.

Marzano, R. J., Pickering, D. J., & Pollock, J. E. (2001). *Classroom Instruction That Works*. Alexandria, VA: Association for Supervision and Curriculum Development.

Noll, J. W. (1997). *Taking Sides: Clashing Views on Controversial Educational Issues*. Guilford, CT: Dushkin/McGraw-Hill.

Peterson, P. E. (1985). *The Politics of School Reform*. Chicago: University of Chicago Press.

Skinner, B.F. (1953). *Science and Human Behavior*. New York: Macmillan.

Skinner, B.F. (1968). *The Technology of Teaching*. New York: Appleton-Centyry-Crofts.

Skinner, B.F., & Epstein, R. (1982). *Skinner for the Classroom: Selected Papers*. Champaign, IL: Research Press.

Vygotsky, L .S., & Cole, M. (1978). *Mind in Society: The Development of Higher Psychological Processes.* Cambridge: Harvard University Press.

Organizations

Center on School, Family, and Community Partnerships
Johns Hopkins University
3003 North Charles Street, Suite 200, Baltimore, MD 21218
410-516-8800
www.csos.com

Communities in Schools
277 South Washington Street, Alexandria, VA 22314
703-518-2557
www.cisnet.org

National Association of Secondary School Principals
1904 Association Drive, Reston, VA 22091
703-860-0200
www.nassp.org

National Community Education Association and the National
Coalition for Parent Involvement in Education
3929 Old Lee Highway, #91-A, Fairfax, VA 22042
703-339-8973
www.ncea.com and www.ncpie.org

Useful Websites

Note: All websites were working at time of writing.

www.adhdsupport.com
www.centerforlearningdifferences.org
www.ci.huntington-beach.ca.us/CityDepartments/fire/search_
    and_Rescue_Explorer_Program

www.jhu.edu
www.ldonline.org/educators
www.learningrx.com
www.life.familyeducation.com
www.nces.ed.gov/programs/coe/press/highlights.asp
www.parentsandschools.net/article.html
www.stophitting.com